MW01097161

Praise for *Time to Get Real*

"A hand of steel in a velvet glove is the best way to describe Julie's journey. A must-read."
—Diane von Fürstenberg

"Creating a tsunami in the fashion business is never easy. Julie managed to create a brand-new retail system to change the buying habits of high-end consumers. A genius modernization of how, when, and where people shop for the best products!"
—Tommy Hilfiger

"I could not put the book down because I watched from the sidelines as this visionary built an entirely new business model under the overwhelmingly misogynistic tech field. I remember meeting her at a *Financial Times* conference and I felt so honored that she knew *me*. What a badass as she controlled the room, fought back the bullies, and went up against some of the big luxury players who tried to stop her. We would not be anywhere in resale or sustainability if it was not for her genius. I am proud to call her my friend."
—Daniella Vitale, CEO of Salvatore Ferragamo

"*Time to Get Real* is an insightful and inspiring read for any entrepreneur or business leader. Julie's journey, from working out of her home to ultimately taking her company public at a billion-dollar valuation, offers not just practical advice, but also a rare look into what it takes to build something truly transformative. This book is a testament to the power of innovation, hard work, and staying true to your vision."
—Congressman Ro Khanna

"Julie Wainwright's debut book is a beautifully inspiring and powerful look into the world of entrepreneurship, innovation, and perseverance. Julie changed the way women shop by making luxury resale not only accessible but also a more earth-friendly, sustainable option. As a woman in tech, Julie's journey is a testament to breaking barriers and leading with vision in an industry often dominated by men. In this book, she shares the highs and lows of building a groundbreaking business from the beginning, offering invaluable lessons learned along the way. This book is an entertaining must-read for entrepreneurs, women in business, and anyone interested in sustainability and the power of reinvention."

—Julie Gilhart, founder and president of GILHART & Co.

"Funny, tough, generous, and honest, Julie Wainwright is every woman's ideal boss and any female entrepreneur's North Star. Part tell-all memoir, part how-to playbook, *Time to Get Real* is a page-turner that disrupts the business-book genre—just like The RealReal disrupted the global fashion system."

—Amy Fine Collins, editor-at-large at Air Mail

"Julie is a force of nature. She combined her knowledge of luxury products, brand affinities, and e-commerce to start The RealReal and then grow it into a public company. Today, The RealReal is the world's largest luxury consignment marketplace because of Julie Wainwright and her resilience."

—Maha Ibrahim, general partner at Canaan Partners

"In a world of deepfakes, Julie Wainwright is the rare authentic deal. If you are a founder who wants to know what happens for real on the journey to build a category winner, this is the book for you."

—**Keval Desai, founder of SHAKTI VC**

"True resilience is not just rising after the fall; it's daring to rebuild on your own terms. Julie created not just a company in The RealReal, but a legacy that no one can take away."

—**Ann Winblad, founder partner of Hummer Winblad Venture Partners**

"I absolutely love this book. Julie's entrepreneurial journey is nothing short of inspiring. She demonstrates how, through hard work, passion, and unwavering optimism, it's possible to go against the odds and to turn adversity into triumph and transform setbacks into true success. I highly recommend this book to every entrepreneur."

—**Payam Zamani,** *USA Today* **bestselling author of** *Crossing the Desert*

Time to
Get Real

Time to Get Real

How I Built a Billion-Dollar Business That Rocked the Fashion Industry

Julie Wainwright

Founder and Former CEO of **THE REALREAL**

BenBella Books, Inc.
Dallas, TX

Disclaimer: This memoir is based on the author's personal experiences, notes, and recollections. To protect the privacy of individuals mentioned, some names and identifying details have been changed or omitted. Dialogue presented in this book reflects the author's best recollection of conversations and is intended to convey the essence of those interactions. The events and experiences described are subjective and should be understood within the context of the author's perspective.

Time to Get Real copyright © 2025 by Julia Wainwright

BenBella
BenBella Books, Inc.
8080 N. Central Expressway
Suite 1700
Dallas, TX 75206
benbellabooks.com
Send feedback to feedback@benbellabooks.com

BenBella is a federally registered trademark.

Printed in the United States of America
10 9 8 7 6 5 4 3 2 1

Library of Congress Control Number: 2024057548
ISBN 9781637746868 (hardcover)
ISBN 9781637746875 (ebook)

Editing by Camille Cline and Victoria Carmody
Copyediting by Jessica Easto
Proofreading by Ashley Casteel and Denise Pangia
Text design and composition by Aaron Edmiston
Cover design by Morgan Carr
Printed by Lake Book Manufacturing

Special discounts for bulk sales are available.
Please contact bulkorders@benbellabooks.com.

This book is dedicated to my father, who started his own business at the age of twenty-eight with four young children and a very sick wife to care for. His passion for creating something new every day, his curiosity, and his humor inspire me to this day.

It is also for my dear friend, Kathryn, who fought one cancer after another and sadly left us in late 2023.

And it is for every entrepreneur who takes a risk to believe in themselves and to create a business against all odds.

Contents

Preface

Without leaps of imagination, or dreaming, we lose the excitement of possibilities. Dreaming, after all, is a form of planning.

—Gloria Steinem

My father told me this story: When I was three years old, we lived on a lake near Kalamazoo, Michigan. My father's favorite way to relax after work and show off was to water-ski around the lake a few times, still in his suit and tie. One summer evening when he was having his hot dog moment on his trick skis, he saw me wandering down the dock with every doll I owned cradled in my arms. My mom was nowhere in sight. He watched as I walked right off the end of the dock. All he could see were my dolls floating away. Somehow, he signaled to the boat driver to get him back on land. He was sure I had drowned. Screaming for my mother, he raced down the dock and looked over its edge. What he saw was me looking back at him. I had pulled myself up and was clinging to a lower board under the dock.

I am not sure why he told me this story when I was in my fifties, except maybe to remind me that, even as a toddler, I found a way to save myself. And maybe he wanted me to know that we all have everything we need inside ourselves to move forward in life despite what knocks us down.

Why am I sharing this anecdote?

It speaks to defying the odds, which every entrepreneur does. This is an entrepreneur's story.

———

Here's a little bit about me. I was born to two artists. My mother and father met at the Chicago Academy of Fine Arts College in the 1950s. My mother wanted to be a fashion illustrator. My father wanted to open his own art and design business. My mother dropped out of college to marry my father and, after a very rough start to their marriage, ended up having four children by the age of twenty-eight. I am the oldest. My father opened his own art and design business before he turned thirty. My mother's life was pretty much over around the same time. She became ill after giving birth to her fourth child, my sister Sherry, and was hospitalized for a while. We, meaning mostly me since the other children were too young to understand, were told by my father that she was dying. I was eight years old. He asked me to step up and help take care of the family. My mother didn't die then, and it took another eight years of strange symptoms to accurately diagnose her with multiple sclerosis (MS). There were minimal ways to treat MS at that time, and they mostly centered around pumping a person full of cortisone. My mother was in a wheelchair in her forties and was put in a twenty-four-hour care facility in her early fifties. When she died at the age of sixty-two, she was a shell of a person. She had advanced dementia, her bones were protruding and mangled, and only once in a while did she recognize any of us. She seemed mostly scared.

Before she slipped away from us, it wasn't all sad times. My father and mother liked to find their fun. We all had motorcycles, which we rode mostly off road, and we had a few go-carts to race around the driveway. My father had an annual badminton tournament that morphed into a tennis tournament after a few years. He designed custom Wainwright Invitational T-shirts for the players. We made our own wine with labels designed by both parents. The wine probably was undrinkable, but the labels were cool. We went on fun vacations every summer until my mother was unable to do so. We laughed a lot, and I developed a somewhat dark sense of humor.

My father loved his business, and I loved hearing about it. His clients were mostly national brands, like Kohler, Flintstones vitamins, Alka-Seltzer, Studebaker, and his favorite, the University of Notre Dame. He had a small team of artists on payroll and a partner who was a very good graphic designer. My father was the main salesperson for his firm, Wainwright Raber, and a great illustrator. He enjoyed talking about what was "on the boards," how his company's designs solved marketing problems. And he thoroughly enjoyed showing all of us the Easter eggs he put in the crowd scenes.

When I look back at my life, my mother's MS clearly had a significant impact on me. Beyond giving me the gift of resilience, it also had a profound impact on my college choice and my first major choice. I applied to Purdue University and was accepted before I started my senior year of high school. Why Purdue? I wanted to study pharmacy and drug development. Somewhere in my psyche was a buried desire to help find a cure for MS for my mom and others with this horrible disease. It sounds like it was a conscious decision, but it was not. Drug development felt creative and important. And I was good at math and science. This decision was bound tightly to another unconscious decision: I did not want to be an artist and compete with my father. And yet, I had talent as an artist. From a young age, I had been painting and drawing daily. At the age of twelve, I was shepherded into a young artists' program at Indiana University's extension school in South Bend, which took place in the evenings.

So, off to Purdue University I went to dive into the study of pharmacy. After a year of classes, I decided that pharmacy was not for me. I didn't want to work in a retail environment, meaning a drug store, and even though I loved chemistry, especially organic chemistry, I neither wanted to get my PhD in biochemistry nor stay in school that long.

During this time, I was also involved with a young man who was a graduate student. He had an undergrad degree in agriculture and was working on his master's degree in business. We met the first day I arrived at Purdue and started dating soon after that. It took a couple of years for him to confess that he had paid someone to get my class schedule and was stalking me. This made total sense once he confessed because we kept running into each other almost daily . . . a hard thing to do in a school with thirty thousand students. It feels creepy now, but at the time, I was impressed with his initiative. He said it was love at first sight when we met.

This man and I ended up getting engaged during my sophomore year. During that year, I was also trying to pick a new major. I wanted something that I loved and was good at. I was also doing his graduate-level marketing homework, as he was struggling. He kept getting As on my work. And I loved the classwork. I had found my calling and would soon change my major to business.

Just like my mother before me, I dropped out of college after my sophomore year to get married. Unlike my mother, I planned to go back to college once my fiancé completed his graduate studies and was settled in his new position. So, in May 1977 after completing my Spring courses at Purdue, I rented a small apartment in Carmel, Indiana, to be closer to him and his family. I wanted to make some money prior to our November wedding, and his father made me an offer I could not refuse: a position working for Delco Remy, a General Motors manufacturing plant, riveting Monte Carlo rear bumpers. And, with that position, I would be joining the United Auto Workers, Local 663. His father was general manager of the plant, and this plant was deploying new technologies to make the first polyurethane/soft bumpers. They had lots of manufacturing issues bringing these bumpers to the market, and they needed extra labor. So, I took a position as bumper riveter on the line. I stayed in the job nearly six months. During this time, when my fiancé's father would explain the challenges of introducing new technologies and shop floor automation, then discuss the solutions they were attempting. Learning from him was an incredible experience, and while I knew I didn't want to go into manufacturing as a businessperson, I loved the complexity of it.

I never did get married. I called off the wedding about thirty days before it was supposed to take place. For a week, I walked the wedding invitations to the mailbox and just couldn't put them in. I kept feeling that my life would get too small if I married that young.

After I called off my wedding, I re-enrolled at Purdue with a new designated major, business with an emphasis in marketing. I soon realized that I had been in marketing training all of my young life. My dad had been indirectly training me on consumer marketing. He would often bring home examples of consumer packages or sales promotional artwork that his business had done. Then he would discuss why these designs worked or didn't work once in the market. Meaning, the new package, for example, either increased sales or it didn't, and he explained the key reasons for the results. This served me exceedingly well once I was back in college.

I took as many graduate-level classes as I could and was excelling in almost all of them. My professor of consumer psychology said he had never met anyone like me, and he emphasized that I was far ahead of the class and better than any student he had taught. I loved his class and felt like everything he was teaching was common sense. Most likely, I had come to the class with the magical ten thousand hours of learning about consumer marketing from conversations with my father. This professor helped me secure my first job, at Clorox in brand management. I was only the second undergraduate they had ever hired. I started in January 1980.

After nearly three years at Clorox, I left for the personal computer software industry and never looked back. I joined Software Publishing Corporation, one of the first companies in personal computer software. When I resigned from Clorox, the general manager said something like, "I could raise the price of Clorox bleach by half a cent and make more money than Software Publishing will in three years." My reply: "Okay, well, I'm young, and if it's a mistake, I'll figure something out."

Software Publishing was an amazing opportunity for me. Within three years of joining the company, I had moved to London to set up the international division for the company. This position required me to create partnerships for codevelopment and marketing around the world. I was in Paris, Munich, Milan, and Barcelona weekly, and I traveled to Singapore, Hong Kong, Taipei, Auckland, and Sydney every quarter. My immediate supervisor was let go, so getting the international business launched and growing was left to me. This position honed my ability to set the right priorities for the best results. It also broadened my worldview.

I was living in London in my late twenties and early thirties during this six-year period. I also was keenly aware that I needed to decide whether I wanted to have children; the proverbial clock was ticking. My first step: I made a conscious decision to date, which at first seemed more like real work and less fun than the work I was doing. Then something clicked, and having a partner and maybe having children, my own family, became a priority for me. I made time to date and meet new people. I met my future husband through friends when I was thirty-one. Within two years, we had married in London and soon thereafter relocated to the United States.

After we left London, we settled down in Northern California. I worked as vice president of sales and marketing at Berkeley Systems, the originator of the Flying Toasters screensaver and, eventually, You Don't Know Jack, the bestselling game of the year in the late 1990s. I was soon promoted to president and then CEO there. After the company was sold, I joined Reel.com, the first company to sell movies online, as the CEO. Once that was sold, I was asked to take the reins of a new e-commerce company, a start-up. A young founder was running this new company out of his apartment in Los Angeles. The year was 1998, and the company was Pets.com.

Pets.com was a website that sold pets supplies, one of the first and certainly the best funded. Think Chewy.com but better and twenty years earlier. (I might be a little biased.) Pets.com rose to fame because of its great puppet mascot and television commercials, especially the ad that ran during the Super Bowl in 2000. That ad was voted the best of the Super Bowl by USA Today and helped accelerate sales. With mismatched button eyes, safety pins holding its ears on, and a Timex watch for a collar, the sock puppet became a celebrity, thanks to its charming, and sometimes naughty, personality. The puppeteer's arm was visible throughout the commercials. Voiced by actor/comedian Michael Ian Black, it was funny and irreverent. It was a crazy time in the internet world with many business-to-consumer companies being funded because of the rise of Amazon.com.

I took Pets.com public in early 2000. By the end of 2000, I was shutting the company down and returning money to shareholders after paying off our liabilities. I did this because the industry was facing a moment when unprofitable companies could no longer get funded. Pets.com needed to raise about $100,000,000 to reach profitability. The funding dried up quickly after Amazon, as a public company, reported a loss of nearly $900,000,000 in the last quarter of 1999. The markets and the technology investors went from rewarding those companies that spent to establish prominence and gain market share, known as a land grab, to expecting instant profitability. The market felt like it changed overnight, and the funding window closed. Pets.com was about twenty-four months from profitability, and I didn't see a way to bridge our need for funding. After consultations with the board, bankers, and the SEC, I shut the company down. Over one thousand companies folded over the next twelve months. Those one thousand companies included a company called Webvan, the precursor to Insta-cart. Webvan had raised more than $1 billion and had burned through all its cash by the time it shuttered its doors. It lost the most amount of investor dollars ever experienced in the venture world by a factor of at least two times. But despite this, Pets.com became the symbol of dot-com craziness.

In fact, the Pets.com's puppet and the company became the face of the dot-com bust. And I became persona non grata in the technology industry. Some chat boards and one pundit called me the dumbest person in the industry. My husband asked for a divorce during this time. He picked the day I was shutting down Pets.com to leave me. I was shattered.

I was forty-two years old. I did not have children, but not because I hadn't tried. I just wasn't committed enough to try extraordinary measures. After my husband left, I had to make a hard decision fast. Have a child on my own or not have children at all. I decided after many discussions with friends and therapists not to have children. That was a tough decision that still makes me sad at times, but I still believe it was the right one. I couldn't have imagined how difficult my life was about to become. Having a child would have added tremendous pressure. Or at least it felt that way at the time.

Pets.com defined my career in a way I could not have imagined. It was a failure, and the technology industry does not like failures, especially public failures.

I let it define me until I didn't.

What I didn't realize until years later was that experience, that big public failure, had oddly freed me from worrying about failing again. I had lived through those disasters, and if I failed again, I'd survive again. I hadn't started my own business before because I was afraid of failing. Now that fear was gone. It had evaporated. And so did my opinion that the entrepreneurs getting funded for their start-ups were all brilliant, much smarter than me. My early image of myself was that I was just the person to operationalize a founder's brilliant ideas. I also thought that I still had so much to learn before I could start my own business. Both were excuses for my fear.

Here's what you need to consider: If I could start a business at the age of fifty-two, you can, too. You, too, can go against the odds.

And it certainly does not have to be within the venture capital system. However, that is how I funded The RealReal, and it worked for me despite the odds.

If this book helps you understand that and inspires you, mission accomplished.

This is the story of The RealReal, a company that changed the fashion industry, changed perceptions of wearing previously owned items, and raised awareness about the importance of recirculating goods for the environment. This is the story of a company that I started in my kitchen, dining room, living room, almost every room in my house, and built to over $1 billion in top-line revenue.

Chapter 1

The Truth Hurts

I sat down with my three dogs—Betty, Louie, and Mo—on either side of me, a glass of wine in my hand, and stared out to Angel Island and Raccoon Straits as the fog rolled in over the Bay. I was looking for my next gig and had just come from a meeting with a tech recruiter, who I'll call Mr. Cupid. To put it mildly, I got no love from Mr. Cupid. I asked him why every opportunity that came my way was horrible, simply the dregs. Each company was a turnaround. The quality of their teams was poor, and the quality of the venture capitalists investing in them was just as bad. He looked me squarely in the eyes and said something like, "You are only as good as your last gig, and your last gig was horrible. You are close to being unemployable in the Valley." I was so shocked at his candor that I don't even remember exactly how I responded. All I remember saying was that Pets.com was years ago, and he said, "And what success have you had since then?"

I don't remember how I got home, either. Clearly, I drove myself because my car was in the carport when I went out the next morning, and Uber hadn't been invented yet.

I could not escape what had happened nearly ten years before. On one single day, everything changed. On that day, I shut down Pets.com.

Mr. Cupid made it clear that my career in Silicon Valley was over. On some level, he said, I was clearly deluding myself to think I could still get a good CEO position in the industry. He set me straight, it was not going to happen. I might be offered a turnaround.

He said what I knew to be true. I didn't want it to be so, but he verbalized my reality and reinforced my fears. The clarity smacked me in the face. I could not waste more time and burn through more money. I had to do something different.

I simply couldn't go on more interviews for positions that would suck my soul out of my body. I knew I was done with that phase of my life. But where to go next? I had tremendous energy, was extremely healthy, had deep experience, and knew how to get the most important things done and hire great teams. Yet none of what I had to offer seemed to be of value to early-stage companies or, more significantly, to their investors.

As is the case for many women, my career progression in technology positions had always been hard. The only reason I had risen to the level of CEO was because I had joined a company that was failing, and I developed a plan to turn that company around—and it worked. That company was the software innovator Berkeley Systems. If my plan hadn't worked, I wouldn't have had any future CEO opportunities. But it did work, and I happily took my next job as the CEO of Reel.com, the first site to rent movies online. That business had a successful outcome for investors, and I was offered my next CEO opportunity, to be CEO of Pets.com, the online purveyors of pet supplies. And that is when the music stopped.

I called my friend Kathryn later that Friday night. Could she hike Mount Tam with me tomorrow? I really needed to talk to her. I needed her perspective. Kathryn had worked with me at Berkeley Systems and Pets.com. She knew me well, and I knew she would be honest. We met in the parking lot by the horse stables at a trailhead in Mount Tamalpais State Park in Marin County, not far from my house on Belvedere Island. The air was crisp, and the hike was strenuous and straight up. But the payoff was worth it. The views at the top were of San Francisco, the Golden Gate Bridge, Sausalito, Tiburon, San Rafael, and the Richmond–San Rafael Bridge.

"So, what choices do you have?" Kathryn asked as we headed up the trail.

"Start my own company or move to Arizona and sell real estate and become a yoga instructor."

"You hate yoga."

"Hate is a strong word. It just feels like a cult."

"Do you have any ideas for a new business?"

"Nothing," I told her.

"I know you can start your own company. You're a good leader. You can do it. The industry is brutal to women. So what! You have never let that stop you before. I know it can be odd and isolating being the only woman in the room. I know when we fail as women, we fall further and beat ourselves up longer. I also know how you run and build companies. You can do this."

"I guess I'll have to figure it out. Or I won't. But I have to try. At some point, I am going to run out of money."

"Yep, that is a concern. Money is important," she said. "The divorce hurt, I know. Giving away half of what you worked for feels wrong, especially when your husband didn't financially contribute. I've been there, I know."

I appreciated her sympathy and understanding. It's what I needed to hear.

"Money is a big concern. I'll have to give myself a timeline for success." As we rounded a curve in the path, I added, "I need to go home and develop a framework before I take some action. I did the math. I'm going to run out of money in less than two years. That is a long time on some level. And really scary on another level. I don't have the luxury of finding my way toward success. I am going to have to nail it."

"You need to try," she said reassuringly.

I could not imagine that, within the next two years, I would be starting on the journey of a lifetime. All I knew is that I couldn't keep doing what I had been doing.

Chapter 2

From Oh No to Oh Yeah

I started on my business journey in the fall of 2010, ten years after the dot-com bust. The dot-com bust was in 2000. That was followed by the terrorist attack on the Twin Towers on September 11, 2001. Both events created an economic shock, but it was nothing compared to the 2008 collapse of the home-lending market. That collapse led to a great recession in the United States and worldwide. More than eight million jobs disappeared overnight. People lost their homes because of increasing interest rates. The economic shock had a long tail, and by late 2010, the US economy was slowly pulling out of one of the toughest economic times it had experienced since the Great Depression. And I was slowly pulling out of my own personal tailspin, highly aware that my cash runway wasn't very long.

It was prudent for me to consider a plan B. It was pragmatic, although bleak. Whatever plan A I came up with, I realized it would have to be completely different from the career I had known for more than twenty-five years, being a gun-for-hire in an exciting, well-funded company. I knew deep down that I had to try starting my own company. I loved entrepreneurs. I loved their start-up stories. I admired them. I wanted to be one of them because they charted their own course. They knew what they were made of, and they believed in themselves.

I knew for sure that I wanted to get back into e-commerce. I love hearing the cash register ring. It's thrilling to know that people are buying what you are selling. I believed I had a deep understanding of consumer psychology, specifically what motivates someone to do something. Fortunately, the cost of testing a concept and getting a business going had dropped considerably over the last ten years.

In 1999, when I took over Pets.com, setting up a server farm and writing code for the required software were extensive and expensive. You could have easily sunk $3 to $5 million into a prospective business before you even opened your virtual doors. We did burn close to that amount of capital at Pets.com. The arrival of open-source software, whereby engineers share their source code, allowed for an exponentially quicker and more efficient development of software. But as open-source software was still in its infancy in 1999, every piece of code for Pets.com had to be original. Before then, engineers everywhere were writing similar code to do similar things. Once the open-source mentality was adopted, it accelerated the personal computer software industry immeasurably, although of course, initially, no large company wanted to participate or allow their engineers to share code. Now it was 2010, and I was pretty sure I could get a site up for between $100,000 and $200,000, a fraction of the software and hardware costs of 1999. This meant I could get going and test a concept without outside funding.

The big question was: What could I do that was distinct and salient to consumers?

I knew it had to be something that Amazon could not do. So, I developed a list of things Amazon could not do. That list was short.

Amazon hadn't shown the ability to develop branded products that could be sold on its platform. This had to be an opportunity. Whatever I did, I knew that I would focus on branded products with a higher perceived intrinsic value than that product's actual cost. Under this heading, I had three product categories that were interesting to me and better for people or the planet. The first was organic makeup and its adjacent category, organic hair products. I had lived in the United Kingdom when it was part of the European Union, and I understood the strict regulations for any ingredient that goes on or in your body. Makeup and hair products in Europe had far fewer carcinogens than any products manufactured for the US market. This made them less effective but, in theory, safer. I wondered if a truly organic makeup or hair-product line could be formulated for the US market and then sold directly to the consumer.

Along the same lines, I thought about cleaning products. I had deep knowledge of the space from my days at Clorox in its cleaning products division. Only one brand, Seventh Generation, was staking the earth-friendly claim at that time in the United States. Surely, there was room for another.

Finally, I was aware that Amazon could not sell luxury products on its platform.

These three areas were the only ones on the short list for my potential new venture. Meanwhile, to hedge my bets, I put my house up for sale. The Arizona yoga plan was still in play. The housing market was in a slump due to the savings-and-loan collapse, so I figured it might take more than a year to sell my house, by which time I would have depleted half my cash. I was always doing the cash-in-hand math.

With my house sitting on the market, my next step was to explore each of the areas that I had identified. I quickly dismissed the luxury category because I wasn't about to start a new luxury brand. Diving deeper into the organic makeup line concept took more time. There were several makeup companies that produce brands for others with labs that anyone with capital can leverage. They developed to your specification and had in-depth knowledge of the ingredients and the chemistry for each type of product. In discussions with a lab, it became clear to me that makeup wouldn't be shelf stable without nonorganic chemicals in them. So, although one could claim their product had "natural" ingredients, truly organic was impossible. And "natural" was such an unregulated term that it could easily be bastardized by anyone. Also, this is a category that has a low barrier to entry. With another $50,000, I could test a series of products—but so could anyone else, and I didn't have a hook. I didn't have a way to enter the market that was unique, differentiated, salient, and defensible and that had large potential. These are the most important components for any new business to succeed. I hadn't totally given up on the makeup and hair product categories, but I didn't see a way to win.

My next investigation led more deeply into good-for-the-planet, safe-for-the-user cleaning products. I tried the existing products on the market, including the Method line that had suddenly shot to fame and success. I loved that brand, but it wasn't claiming anything special. It was seemingly safer to the consumer and packaged in much cooler bottles, but it did not claim to be organic or natural.

So, where to go next? I was now ambling into late October. There were only a few people interested in seeing my house. The recession of 2008's long tail was not my friend. It was a buyer's market.

I was certainly concerned but not worried yet. I loved a good Gordian knot, and I still had time. Having plan B underway gave me some comfort and a lot of motivation because I hated plan B.

October rolled into November. By then, I had decided that none of my original plan A ideas would work easily, if at all. I still wasn't panicked. I kept thinking I should be. What made me anxious was thinking I should be anxious, and I wasn't.

And then, while I was shopping with a friend, the light bulb switched on. The concept literally came together in a split second.

My friend and I were shopping in her friend's boutique in Menlo Park. The store had top new luxury shoe brands like Louboutin and Fendi in the front and an area in the back called The Vault. The Vault was stocked with beautifully merchandised, consigned luxury goods. There were some Chanel suits, some Louis Vuitton and Gucci handbags. Elegantly styled mannequins displayed Alexander McQueen and Alaïa dresses. Vintage Saint Laurent baubles were enticingly arranged along with Chanel earrings and necklaces in glass jewelry cases.

Much to my amazement, my friend spent the whole time shopping in The Vault. We had shopped together many times before, and I had never seen her buy resale. Once we stepped out of the boutique, I began interrogating her.

Had she ever shopped in a consignment store before?

"No," she stated firmly. "I never would. They smell, and I don't want to sort through the racks to find the really nice things."

Would she ever shop on eBay?

"No, too many fakes."

Had she ever consigned?

"No, too hard." She gave things to her sister or put things in storage.

Then why did she buy resale now?

"Everything is beautiful in this store. I trust the owner that these are not fake. Everyone likes a deal on Chanel, Louis Vuitton, and Gucci."

Boom! It was like a lightning bolt. I had it. The idea I had been looking for. From there, the business crystallized quickly. The luxury market was my category. I had already researched it and knew the primary luxury market earned more than $200 billion worldwide, historically showed fast rebounds after recessions, and had great growth numbers. Now, I just needed to research the existing competition in the resale market and look in my own closet to see if I had any luxury goods to consign.

Here's what I knew from the excursion to the boutique with The Vault. First, the luxury resale items were all beautifully merchandised as if they were new. Luxury brands spend millions of dollars each year to transport the buyer to a world of glamour and sophistication. They tell you a big, aspirational story. The owner of the boutique had preserved that fantasy with the clever way she presented each item. I called it "keeping the romance alive." My new business would have to keep the romance alive, too. I knew I would need a merchant to do this. I'm not a merchant, but I thought I would know one when I saw one.

Second, the items were priced about 40 percent off the original retail price. It felt like a real deal. Resale had to be a great value. I understood that, over time, the marketplace would set the price and that my new company would set the price based on the marketplace. Consumers could not set their own prices. This would be an interesting tactic, never attempted online before. For example, eBay's posters always set their prices. If I allowed this in my new company, nothing would ever sell. Suppose you bought, for example, an Armani gown for $3,500, which is a lot of money. You might think you could sell it for $3,200 if you had only worn it once. But what if no one would pay you that amount for the dress? How long would you keep the price at $3,200? What if someone else wanted to sell the same dress for $500 and it sold in forty days? Would you even know that was the price point that people are willing to pay? You would not. But by setting up the database and data tags correctly, the new business would know the optimal price.

The beauty of an aggregation of buyers on the internet is that they will vote for the correct price with their dollars. The average person doesn't have access to that kind of data. But I knew my new company would over time. The data would allow the company to price things to sell within a ninety-day window. The data would also indicate the trends of a brand. Controlling the price and using data to set the price would also keep people consigning because when their things sold quickly, in theory, they would be encouraged to keep consigning. This should have the critical effect of keeping inventory levels low at the operations centers. Controlling pricing would also allow the new company to be transparent about what brands are hot and what brands are not.

For example, basic Armani garments have not been hot since the formation of The RealReal. In this instance, Armani was being resold in other places for pennies on the dollar when I started The RealReal. Someone would be lucky to get $500 for an Armani women's suit, originally priced at $2,500. This is not a reflection of the designer's talent—it is only a reflection of what people are willing to pay for it in the secondary market. The online reseller marketplace is the truth teller.

In the beginning, I would not have a deep dataset of information, so I would have to price against a known quantity, which at that time meant eBay. Pricing slightly less than a consignment store or eBay would be my entry point. Competitive pricing combined with a higher commission rate for the consignor would presumably encourage both the supply and demand sides of the marketplace. The resale items in the Menlo Park boutique were in very good condition. No odors and few marks on the interior or exterior of handbags. Condition was crucial, so there would be smaller rejections of consigned items. I knew I needed to solve that problem upfront.

The last and maybe most important factor for success had to be trust. Trust was imperative. My friend trusted the owner not to sell fakes and to take care of her if she was unhappy. My new company had to engender trust and establish a system for authentication. I needed to see how difficult the process was and how I could make it easier. It was clear that I would be building a service company, and I had to reduce the friction and figure out how to obtain the most desirable product easily. Ultimately, though, my idea was all about the product, and I needed a product acquisition strategy.

When I returned home that same afternoon, I wrote down everything that I had observed along with the outline of the key differentiators that would eventually result in The RealReal.

My first step was to see what I had to consign. To my surprise, I had over sixty (sixty!) things in my own closet that I wasn't using and would qualify as luxury items. From shoes to clothes to handbags to jewelry, they were all dust magnets languishing in the back of the closet. I decided to take a few pieces out and use them to sample the competition.

I tried local consignment stores, eBay, and for the jewelry, pawnshops. I tried them in several cities. It was as if the business owners all had the same handbook on how to do things badly and still make money. Local consignment stores made it easy to drop off your items, but hard to get paid, and even harder to track what was happening. And, of course, since these resale stores were dependent on walk-in traffic, the merchandise moved more slowly. The internet, in my business, would eliminate that problem.

Some of these places had an unpleasant smell, and none offered a great shopping experience. A store on Polk Street near Broadway in San Francisco even had an attitude, as if it was a rarefied luxury boutique. So did the handbag resale store on Union Square. The attitude there was elitist and oddly somewhat sinister at the same time. Its sinister atmosphere was exacerbated by the tall guy in a raincoat who walked up to the cashier, collected a large amount of cash, stuffed it into a paper bag, and left. Maybe that is how they did their bank deposits, but it looked pretty sketchy to me.

Next, there was eBay. I tried both an eBay consolidator and self-posting. Neither were good experiences, with slow sell-through and not great pricing. Working though the consolidator provided some convenience, but its service was sluggish, its communication was poor, and it took a big cut of the sales price, nearly 55 percent.

Then came the pawnshops. They were the most trippy and creepy, each one more disgusting than the last. One did look promising, though. It advertised an elevated experience for customers selling fine jewelry and handbags. But then I went there. I was buzzed into a small alcove-like reception area without seats. A woman emerged from a door behind the alcove and beckoned me into the room she had just exited, a windowless cell illuminated by an overhead neon light. I was asked to sit against the wall, in a shabby chair, and I was told the gemologist would be out in a minute. There wasn't one picture on the walls. A wooden side table stained with drink rings held a couple of old magazines. The only other furnishings were a coffee table and another worn-out chair. The resident "gemologist" entered rather quickly. I extracted my Cartier Tank watch from my handbag. It was in its original box, and I opened the box and held the watch with one hand. She grabbed the watch from me and laid it on the table after turning it over and visually inspecting the back. Her first words to me clearly positioned the watch as low in value. This expert made sure that I knew that my watch was no longer in fashion. I had purchased it in 2008, and it was now 2010. Fashion seemed to move quickly in the watch world.

Then she said that smaller women's watches were not worth as much as men's watches. Again, setting expectations that my Cartier watch was a low-value item. She told me that I should have bought a men's Cartier watch. That is what most women wanted to wear now, she said. I said, "Well, this is the watch I have." I asked her if she thought it was worthless, throwing in a "maybe I should leave." She told me she would need to take the watch back to her station to review it more closely. I asked if I could come with her. She said that I could not follow her into that area because it was a security risk. I agreed to have my declining-value Cartier watch taken away and evaluated in another room while I waited in the sordid yellow cell for what seemed like an inordinate amount of time. She could have been switching my watch for a replica for all I knew. I started to get nervous. I have no patience, so it might have been only ten minutes, but it reeked of buying a used car from a disreputable dealer who negotiates in secret with a man behind a curtain. I would have left, but she had my watch, and hopefully I would be getting it back. She reappeared and informed me that she had discussed my Cartier Tank watch with her manager. She placed it on the coffee table near its box. She then wrote the price they would be able to meet on a Post-it. I had paid $5,200 for the watch in 2008. She offered me $2,400. She never said the words—the Post-it did the talking. I asked her if that was her best price. She answered, "Sadly, yes," then reiterated that my watch was out of style. I plucked the watch from the table, fastened it around my wrist, and told her I would consider her offer. Placing the red box in my handbag, I headed to the door. I turned to look at her as I left, and she said she couldn't guarantee that the price wouldn't go down next week.

I felt like I needed a shower after that exchange. Is this what passed for a luxury consignment experience these days? Is this what women had to go through to sell their hard-won or thoughtfully gifted prized possessions? The experiences steeled my resolve to provide a truly VIP interaction.

I knew I could build a much better business than any of the competition. Most important, I knew I had checked off all the boxes for a new business with huge possibilities. I had identified a potentially large market that was Amazon-proof, unique, salient, and consumer facing. People love luxury goods, and I knew that under the right conditions, they would buy them resale. I sensed that the timing was right. The 2008 recession had struck everyone. And the old axiom that everyone likes a bargain was truer now than ever.

I also knew ideas were a dime a dozen. Everyone has ideas. Many young entrepreneurs fight to protect their ideas and think they are so special, and maybe they are. But experience had already taught me that, if I had a great idea, someone somewhere was thinking exactly the same thing at the same time. So, if my idea was going to win in the market, I needed to move fast. Great execution of a solid business idea always wins—especially if others are still thinking about the idea while I was already making it happen. I also recognized that I would be creating a new category on the internet, not trying to steal share from existing businesses. I had been observing and participating in the technology industry for more than twenty-five years and understood the key attributes for category formation:

- It must solve a real problem in a way that is easy for the participants. Reducing friction is important. And it is critical to show real value quickly to the end user.
- It needs to have a previous reference point that feels familiar to the users for faster adoption. Meaning, if it requires too much thinking, it doesn't work well. Or if it is not intuitive to use, it won't get to scale and might end up being an interesting idea that others take to a new level later. Remember my story of riveting Monte Carlo bumpers? The production problems

arose due to a faux metal strip flying off the front bumpers. Why even have these silver, chrome-like strips on the bumper? General Motors's research had shown people liked their metal bumpers. The new soft bumpers had to look like something that resembled chrome.

- It needs to address a big opportunity, also known as a large total available market (TAM), to get funding.
- It requires building a brand with a simple value proposition.
- It requires credibility, which can be reinforced by many things, including the value proposition, the technology, the founder, and the early adopters.
- Timing is critical. For a business looking for funding, the first consideration is timing for opportunity, and the second is timing for the funding. Venture capital funding runs in cycles. Sometimes venture capitalists fund certain categories, and sometimes they do not. And they do tend to follow each other in funding that is primarily driven by their limited partners. Venture capitalists take risks, but they are calculated risks. Fast and good execution is critical. Pets.com was launched as a funding cycle was ending and very early in the internet cycle. Chewy.com was launched twelve years after Pets.com, around the same time as I was launching The RealReal.

I believe the OG of building a new category is Martha Stewart. I would argue she created the first lifestyle brand outside of fashion. Martha turned aspirational entertainment into products. And she did two other key things. First, she made exquisite cooking and at-home entertaining accessible. And here's the most impressive thing: She made it look easy. I will never forget when Martha attended one of the first D conferences, at one time the most important technology conferences, headed by Walt Mossberg and Kara Swisher. Her contribution to the conference gift bags was two cookie sheets, which caused some amused chatter among the attendees. And yet, who else created a lifestyle brand like Martha in the technology world then? Only Apple had strived to be a lifestyle brand. My bet is Apple took a page out of Martha Stewart's marketing playbook whether it knew it or not.

Another great example of someone who built a new category is Anastasia Soare. As a beauty practitioner, she realized that the shape and color of people's eyebrows changed the way their faces looked. I am sure that other practitioners had made the same observation when working with clients. But Anastasia did things differently. She created a brand around eyebrows. She leveraged public relations, technology platforms like Instagram, her Beverly Hills clients and location, and her knowledge to show others that eyebrows make a difference. She developed product lines that excelled in changing the brow line for many, then expanded into other makeup categories. She was the first. She made it easy to look better with small changes to one's daily makeup practice. She literally changed the way people looked at their faces and beauty, then gave them tools that were easy to use to approximate the results she could personally give to her client base. While competition followed, she created a large, successful business and set standards in the industry. She did what large beauty companies had never been able to do. Think about that. All beauty companies had eyebrow products prior to her business, but she created the category.

Another example is Twitter. When it first launched, it provided a simple service where people could get real-time updates on key events happening all over the world. It also had the novelty of removing a wall, so anyone could have direct access to reporters, celebrities, athletes, politicians, and opinion leaders. And its technology mostly worked. There was a point when it seemed like Twitter couldn't scale technically, leaving hundreds of thousands of people disappointed because it went down, meaning it would crash for hours. This happened regularly in the first three years of its existence. If at that time there had been another Twitter-like solution that could scale as a competitor, Twitter would have lost its base.

Another well-known category creator is Uber. It became an easier taxi service and, at some point, was priced competitively with taxis. In Uber's case, if they would have completely stumbled or proved unable to garner further funding, there was a number two waiting in the wings, Lyft. Uber was first, though, and changed transportation worldwide.

One last example may not be as revolutionary as a Twitter or Uber, but it's still relevant. The podcast technology—a new category for the internet—emerged with little fanfare. Usage adoption was slow. It needed content. There were few drivers of great content to speed adoption. Then Marc Maron did something that I can almost guarantee you no venture capitalist would have funded or even thought possible. He started interviewing people, and those interviews were long, over one hour in some cases. He published his content as a podcast. And people started listening. Millions of people. He created the long-form interview category on this new technology platform. So, you have a new platform that enabled a new category.

Building a new category has different characteristics than entering an existing category. Here are the critical factors necessary for entering an established category:

- The product must be significantly better and less expensive than the category leader.
- The product will require a large brand budget or partnership either in the form of a sales team or brand budget to get traction.

- If it is a technology solution, it should work with the brand leader on some level or compete against a business that has low switching costs, meaning the service or product can easily get the company to try another product that is lower in cost.
- It may need to find a niche market in the established category.
- It will still need to get traction quickly.
- The basics apply: It will need the right price, superior product features, great distribution, easily understandable product-market fit, significant competitive advantage, and lots of capital.

I also had to get people to change their behavior and then become loyal repeat customers. This was critical to ensure my new company hit profitability. I had to create both high barriers for entry against the competition while giving the customer/consignor a growing reason to stay loyal. To do this, I needed to create an incentive structure that rewarded staying with the platform, not switching to try others. Since consignors were the most important, we had to reward people who consigned regularly by giving them a better commission structure. The more a person consigned, the more they made. Think of airlines and how they lock you in with air-mile status. It makes switching to another airline difficult. This business needed to make it difficult for a consignor to switch.

Here's an example of a low-switching-cost business: a cupcake company. Who wouldn't want to try a new cupcake? Especially if the price is good and the cupcake looks amazing. The challenge with this type of business is distribution and awareness.

Another business that I believe has a low switching cost is Docu-Sign. Although it was amazing when it was introduced, most businesses could easily switch to a lower-cost product to have their documents signed electronically and securely over email.

My goal was to make switching hard for the consignor.

I wrote a business plan in a PowerPoint presentation. Then I called a lawyer at Sidley Austin to incorporate a new company. It was close to my birthday in early March, and I was alive with excitement and an early consciousness of success. It felt bone good.

I needed a name for the new business. So, I invited two creative friends to join me at the small bar area of Terzo, one of my favorite restaurants in San Francisco. Wine was poured, and we started. I had my laptop with me to see if our name-generation party would yield a name with a URL I could buy. We started with my goal that the name had to engender trust. It had to speak to authenticity, and we needed to separate ourselves from the pack. After several tries and more wine, one of my girlfriends said, "Call it The RealReal." I quickly typed the name in GoDaddy to see if I could buy the URL. Bingo! It was available for $2,500. With a few more clicks, we had a name. The RealReal was christened at Terzo, just before my fifty-second birthday.

Now I had to raise some money—the eternal challenge of any entrepreneur. It is always painful and sometimes revelatory. I developed a pitch and started pitching my friends. My friend Kathryn had committed $100,000 as a personal loan to me. The loan was collateralized with my home, still unsold. A fellow entrepreneur came in at another $100,000. Then the father of the man I was dating committed $50,000. My neighbor, also an entrepreneur, committed $50,000. I had enough to get started as I continued to pitch potential investors. I decided to focus the capital on product acquisition tactics, not on technology. It was and is all about the product. This was a technology-enabled business, not a technology business. It is important to know the difference. It dictates how you spend your money.

The RealReal would launch on an e-commerce platform that was a precursor to Shopify. One Kings Lane, an e-commerce home furnishings company, had used this platform to launch its business, and one of the founders had sung its praises. So, I signed a contract for developing and hosting the website. The RealReal would collect, house, authenticate, pick, pack, and ship all orders from our own warehouse—also known as my house. I called my friend who was the founder of a design company to develop the logo and the brand identity plan. We needed to work within the technology provider's framework, but we could develop the skin for the website.

I also needed a merchant. And maybe a stylist. I started asking friends for recommendations. Another friend suggested a local stylist. Then another friend proposed Rati Sahi, a young woman who owned a designer store on Polk Street and had been recognized on Refinery29 as one of the most progressive retailers in the United States. I met with the local stylist first. I explained the concept and that I could only pay her a small sum of money each month. She was excited and felt her clients would love the service. She signed on to help get the business off the ground. She asked if she could work part time for us as she was reluctant to give up her other job.

Then I met with Rati at her store. She, too, had a back area where she sold consigned luxury goods. We popped over to the corner coffee shop to talk. During our conversation, I had a kind of mystical experience. As I was asking her questions, I saw a movie play on her right shoulder. This vision laid out how the business would grow and how we would work together. I watched the movie play out, and when it ended, I knew she was the correct hire. That is, if she would take the job. I'd had this same type of phantasmagoric vision a couple of times before while contemplating important decisions. That mystical "movie-playing" had never let me down. None of these movies have ever been reruns. They have all been specific to the situation at hand. I honored what I saw as real and knew it was propitious. The Germans have a word for this: *Kopfkino*. It refers to mentally playing out an entire scene in your mind as if in a movie theater. My brain was showing the movies on other people's right shoulders.

I asked Rati to consider shutting down her store and joining me on this venture. She said that 2008 had been a hard year for her retail business, and even though it was 2011, she hadn't fully recovered. She understood the power of the internet and wanted to be part of something bigger than herself. She needed to check with her investors, her parents. Then she added, "I'm still under thirty. I have time to take risks."

Rati called the next day and said she could start in late April but would still need some time to close her store properly. It was late March, and of course, I said yes. I also told her I could pay her only $2,500 a month. Again, she said okay.

I now had a company name. The RealReal was incorporated in the state of Delaware, a technology platform had been identified, a design firm was working on the website and logo, and I had two employees, both of whom would start sometime in April. The stylist would work part time. Rati said she would commit to full time.

The next phase was to secure a warehouse. To save money, I waited and turned my house into an operations center. All furniture in the living room was moved to its far end, packed so tightly that the only place to sit was on the floor. This would be a processing area. I bought some rolling racks and hangers for the clothes. My family room received similar treatment—and that became the photography area. The dining room was converted into the planning room. Then I purchased a mannequin for photography. It was a vintage Adel Rootstein dummy, phenomenally wrong for production work but very chic. Her lifelike form and face were based on a real British ingenue actress from the 1960s, and that spooky verisimilitude triggered a memory from one of my college jobs. I worked at the local department store—the only department store—Loeb's, in Lafayette, Indiana, designing displays and windows for a boss who had worked at Bergdorf in Manhattan. When I graduated and had to leave the job, he showed me a manne-quin he had made to resemble me! It was a taller version of me, and I acted pleased, but I was totally creeped out.

We were ready to go, but I still needed product and a product acquisition strategy. That was paramount. I had called all my friends, asked them to consign with us, and gathered their things. Rati and the stylist did the same. We had about two hundred items ready to be authenticated and then we needed to create a unique stock keeping unit (SKU) to identify each product, work that we did while sitting on my living room floor. A good start, but this clearly wasn't scalable. I needed aggregators, and the best aggregators were stylists.

Stylists tend to work with many high-net-worth clients, and it is not unusual for those clients to spend tens of thousands of dollars a month on clothing. They often are tasked with cleaning out closets and reselling their clients' clothes, beyond helping them buy new cloth-ing. I developed a program whereby the stylist would receive 10 per-cent of the take for the items sold on the soon-to-be launched site. I then worked my connections in Los Angeles for introductions to key stylists. I met maybe ten in April. And then I contacted their agents, makeup experts, anyone who knew anyone who might consign. The RealReal's first affiliate program was born. I bought a direct-mail list with the names and addresses of more stylists and their agencies and sent out an email blast announcing the business.

In my spare time—of which there was none—I started authenti-cating and SKUing. We had worked with the technical provider to add a super field for the consignor's email, which was then connected to multiple products. The following month, we would figure out how to run a report to pay the consignors.

When creating the backend database, we needed a brand and product identifier system and settled on something easy, GU for Gucci, CHA for Chanel, and so on, with SKU numbers following. The brand abbreviations would allow us to run a report quickly to understand how much of each product we had. Clearly, it wasn't hard in my house to figure out quantities of any given brand, but when you envision hundreds of thousands of SKUs, these easy IDs would certainly help. And I was envisioning a big business.

I expected I would have unlimited demand. I just needed a repeatable product strategy. The affiliate program was a good place to start, but it was insufficient. I was considering hiring a sales team to go to people's homes to pick up product. Of course, I couldn't pay them yet, but that was clearly the direction I was heading because we were all bringing in product to my living room anyway.

We also needed a photographer who was game for an adventure without a lot of pay. We found a young guy with his own camera, and we invested in some professional lights, seamless white paper, and a white paper rack stand.

And I found a friend, Mary, who said she could come over and help us SKU and authenticate products in her spare time for free. Mary is funny, pays great attention to detail, and sometimes bursts into song without prompting or context. It is weird, hilarious, and comforting all at the same time when it first happens. By the next time, you just get on with your work while Mary does her thing. Mary is a frustrated opera singer. She studied voice in college and then went into technology, working for AOL. She had a limited but captive audience in my house. Even my dogs enjoyed her warbling. Meanwhile, Rati, the stylist, and the photographer worked almost for free, too.

My house was taken over by The RealReal. My life was, too. My boyfriend was living with me at the time, and he was getting grumpy. Rati had commandeered the refrigerator and kitchen counter.

The team had been in my house for less than four weeks. It was kind of fun but, again, not scalable. There was a theme going on here. We needed more space, more employees, and better processes, and I needed more sleep. The last one was hard to come by. But for the other three, just expanding out of my house would be a good place to start.

Fixing the "my house is the warehouse" problem was easy. I needed to find a warehouse before we opened our virtual doors for our first sale to consumers on June 10. I called my commercial real estate broker friend who was part of my "name the company" team for help. Even though she normally handles multimillion-dollar contracts, I asked her to find us a warehouse in Marin County for less than $35,000 a year. I told her we needed a room for an office, another area to SKU the product, and a photography space that could double as a waystation for shipments. Miraculously, she did it.

We moved into the 2,500-square-foot end unit of an odd mixed-use small business development area in the Canal Area of San Rafael in Marin County. This district was known for sex workers, drug dealers, and all kinds of shenanigans. That was the downside, along with its lack of air conditioning, its persistent smell of bacon, and its crunchy brown carpeting that sounded like you were treading on a field of Rice Krispies whenever you entered. The pros were that it was next to a sandwich shop run by a police officer—hence the bacon odor—there was a coffee shop at the end of the little seven-unit complex, the Merry Maids cleaning service was three doors down, we were five minutes from UPS, and it had a storage loft. The landlord required only a twelve-month lease, with three months' rent up front and a personal guarantee. It was almost perfect.

The flow was like a railroad flat—no hallways, just rooms end to end. The front door, which was all glass, covered now with taped-on black trash bags, opened onto the crunchy brown carpet and five Euro-style desks that Rati, Mary, and I assembled one hot June night. We crammed in five six-foot-long rolling dress racks, and we hung on the back wall a large whiteboard to write the weekly sales. After that came the cramped photography studio with a wooden floor and a bathroom whose door had to remain open to take the shots. This was necessary for the proper distance from the mannequin to ensure the entire item was captured. The next section in this warren was an even tighter space that would soon house handbags and shoes in plastic Container Store bins and a desk for the part-time accountant. The layout changed in the warehouse, where we had a long packing table, a big roll-up door at the back, and, above, the storage loft.

The photographer jumped ship before we migrated to San Rafael. I was glad to see him go since I didn't want to keep cleaning up his messes. He splattered pee everywhere in my bathroom, and I retched every time I cleaned up after him. I felt like I had to clean that bathroom daily. You wear many hats in a start-up, including being a janitor. My tolerance as a janitor had its limits.

We needed a new photographer, a hard position to fill. It became Rati's job to find the right person while I shuttled back and forth from Los Angeles to rustle up stylists and explain our story. The local stylist I had hired was still working at her original full-time job and was bringing in product when she could. One day right before we launched, Rati called me while I was hustling in LA. She said the latest photographer had just quit. I think we were on our third or fourth. Most only lasted a couple of hours because they had to dress and undress the mannequin, shoot at least sixty pictures, edit the photos for consistent light, and then crop them—all on the same day. Not exactly anyone's dream job, and it didn't pay that well, either. I simply said to Rati, "Don't you know how to use a camera?" She did, and so she took over until yet another new guy started. He quit soon, too. We would have happily hired a woman, but for some reason, only guys applied.

We finally found a French man who stayed for a few months and did a good job. Like Mary, he sang while he worked. Unlike Mary's arias, Jean-Luc was partial to "Non, je ne regrette rien," one of my favorites. Mary had not made the transition with us to San Rafael, either, and we missed her, not only for her random singing but also for her dramatic health stories. They always started with her having just seen her doctor, who told her she might have something or could develop something that would lead to something else and then she would or could possibly die. She understood these scenarios were absurd, but she couldn't stop herself. Her litanies inadvertently turned into a whole stand-up routine. Rati and I weren't sure if we should laugh, but we did anyway.

At last, our launch day arrived. Rati had laid out sales for the month of June through early July, with a new sale introduced three times a week. We opened our doors on June 11, 2011, and, *hallelujah*, within minutes items were in people's carts! But that is exactly where everything stayed. *No one was completing a sale.* We had cart hoarders. Customers were often stashing fifteen to twenty things in their carts. And those carts were just hanging out on the site without a single transaction. Plus, we had only about one hundred products for sale. This selfish squirreling was totally unexpected and led to instituting the twenty-minute cart timer, still there to this day. Finally, the hoarders released some product, and we finished the day with around $30,000 in sales. Multiply that figure by 30, and then multiply that sum by 12, and you've calculated a $10 million plus run rate. If, of course, we had the product in house.

But we didn't. And I needed to raise more money. Rati's parents had invested about $100,000. And other installments of $25,000 had come in from smaller investors. I was convinced I needed to run a lead-generation program to attract more consignors, but then I'd need at least one person in Los Angeles to pick up the product. In San Rafael, I needed a receiving, copywriting, and authentication team and at least one person to help Rati and me to pick, pack, ship, and answer customer emails.

How to feed this ravenous resale beast? Clearly, without more capital, we were nowhere. I was already working ten hours in the office, and then after dinner I would work at home until I collapsed on my breakfast counter. I was taking Ambien to help me sleep. My mind would not stop.

More than once, I woke up with a ballpoint pen stuck to my face. The dent imprinted on my cheek took hours to disappear. One morning, I woke up with playing cards stuck to my face. It seems I had started playing an Ambien-induced game of solitaire in my sleep. My boyfriend was not amused. I couldn't go on like this, and the only solution was to raise more investment dollars.

Chapter 3

Angels . . . and Other People

W e needed capital, and I knew it was too early to pitch to the venture capitalists. We had not proved our business model. We didn't have great repeat numbers because we did not have enough product flowing into the business that would service our customer base. I needed more time to prove the business model out. And, here's the catch, I needed money to buy me the time.

A new marketplace called AngelList had launched. Entrepreneurs could post their pitch decks on AngelList and match up with smaller investors looking for start-ups in need of funds. I was so excited by this venture that I applied right away to become a verified entrepreneur. AngelList explained that it wanted to curate the opportunities proposed on its platform to make sure that only the most interesting deals were offered. The RealReal was a curated marketplace, so I understood that concept well. We needed capital right after we launched. I applied in May before we even launched the business.

AngelList summarily rejected my application on the grounds that my business was "unsuitable for their investors." I couldn't believe it. The entrenched gender bias in Silicon Valley oozed from its privileged pores. Women tend to attract less than 3 percent of all capital. The guys behind AngelList weren't helping to change that percentage, and they didn't care to. I was determined to find a way around this blatant sex-based discrimination. When I let myself feel the emotions of the constant battle to be seen as a valid businessperson, creating a business that is disruptive and valuable, it exhausted me. The age and gender biases, whether conscious or unconscious, are real. I had been facing it since I started in the workforce at Clorox. But I couldn't let it overwhelm me or wear me down.

I had to keep focused on my goals and move forward. I called my friend who had worked for me as the chief technical officer at Reel .com to complain and see if he had any ideas. He told me that if I got Dave McClure, the founder of the business accelerator 500 Startups, to invest even $25,000, then had him announce on AngelList that he invested in The RealReal, I would be accepted on the platform and probably raise more money. It was a feasible strategy, as I had known Dave McClure before he was a venture capitalist. He had been a contract engineer at Reel.com when I was CEO there.

My former chief technology officer reintroduced me to him, and that started a four-month dance with Dave. Dave was happy to reconnect and said, of course, he would invest $25,000. And once he had done that, he would happily put in a good word for me at AngelList. It turned out, he "just couldn't get to it now" because he was so busy.

That is how VC investors say no. They don't say yes, but they don't say no. Because maybe they could be wrong and maybe they want you to come back later with more results or a better term sheet—a document that lays out all the major deal points for investing in a company—or maybe they just don't want to mess up a future bet. Or maybe they're just wimps.

I went back to my former CTO, and he said he would bug Dave. He reassured me that if Dave said he would invest in The RealReal, he would do it. Maybe he would, but he clearly wasn't on my timeline, which was immediate. The sales challenge is always to have someone embrace your priorities as their own priorities. The tactics are to keep bugging those people in a positive way and do an assumptive close. Every communication assumes they will do what they promised. I was working this angle with Dave, but it was slow. I had to keep knocking on doors and sending emails and making connections at $25,000 a pop. So, that is what I did.

Meanwhile, we were running out of product. My "genius" affiliate plan with stylists seemed to be foundering, too. We needed to spend marketing money and run direct-response campaigns. It's all about the leads, and we didn't have enough of them. If we didn't have product, obviously, we would not have sales, and without sales and a trend line, it is pretty hard to lure investors. Our complete sell-through on a posted sale continued. Our rolling racks and handbag containers were nearly depleted. We were in trouble.

Things were not looking good at our little office in San Rafael. Product was coming in, but slowly. Every sale we ran sold out within minutes. We brought in an intern. We were thinking we'd have to go down to one sale per week until we found a better way to acquire products. Then we got a call from a top Hollywood stylist. The stylist said her client wanted to clean out her warehouses and could we meet her tomorrow. Warehouses—*plural*—full of clothes, shoes, handbags.

Of course, we could be there tomorrow. At least one or two of us would take on the task. Rati and our seventeen-year-old intern took the earliest flight out of San Francisco International Airport to Burbank the next day. The celebrity stylist said to bring a truck. Rati and the intern rented a U-Haul. I stayed back to pick, pack, ship, answer customer service questions, and work on the financing.

I called and texted Rati regularly throughout the day. Did the celebrity really have a warehouse? Yes, she did. Did it look promising? Yes, it did. Was she there? No, they had to bring everything back to her house to make sure that she really wanted to sell everything. Will you be done in a few hours? No. Should I find you a hotel? Yes. Can you send me the intern's home phone number? I will need to call her mom. Sure. You rented what size U-Haul? Can you drive that U-Haul back by yourself, or should I ask my boyfriend to fly down tonight to drive it back? Ask your boyfriend to drive.

My boyfriend got on the plane with toothbrushes and deodorant for them and went right to the hotel. I called the intern's mother, and although she wasn't completely comfortable with her daughter spending the night in LA, she agreed that the intern could stay.

The next morning, I continued trying to get more information on the consignment. I was texting and calling into the black abyss. One-word answers would come back intermittently. No one was giving me any details except that they would be back at the San Rafael warehouse at 7 p.m., latest. This didn't sound good. Or it was good, and Rati was messing with me.

When they arrived close to 7 p.m., Rati jumped out of the truck. She slowly opened the door. The truck was nearly full. They had brought back hundreds of items, mostly clothing but all designers. And even though the celebrity was tiny, there were a lot of size 2, 0, and 00 shoppers out there, and her things sold well. We were going to be okay. We were still in business for a while. That was all that mattered at that moment. One step at a time. One consignor warehouse at a time. The stylist's client was an A-list celebrity and hadn't wanted to run a public sale, so like other consignors, her items were anonymously sold. Her stylist collected her 10 percent as promised.

Other stylists started giving us things at the end of July and into August. We finally had some real traction in Los Angeles. It was clear that it was time for us to hire our first employee in LA. And I was still chasing Dave McClure in August, but the sales of the first celebrity's items had generated a little cash. I had enough capital to start a lead-generation campaign to generate sales opportunities. Once we had real leads, I would look for the employee in LA who was gutsy and smart enough to take this position.

I flew down to LA to interview a few candidates for our first outside sales position. We needed to be ready when people returned from vacation and school started. I set up at a hotel breakfast table and met a couple of candidates. Then I met our future new hire. She was a new mom and had a little baby spit-up on her shoulder, but she was charming and hungry to work again, had luxury marketing and selling experience, and loved the idea of being an entrepreneur in the LA area and doing business development. She was all in! And I offered a whopping $48,000 a year plus a 20 percent bonus. You may recall that Rati was still making $2,500 a month with a promise to go to $5,000 a month at the end of the year if we were hitting our numbers. She was offered stock, though, and so was the first Los Angeles hire. She accepted without hesitation, even though it meant working out of her home—unheard of at the time, and of course, she had no idea she would be sorting consignor items on her dining room table for nearly a year before we opened our first office.

So, now I needed a bonus plan that rewarded the right behavior. All luxury brands are not the same in resale value. And we didn't want to get bogged down with rejections. What I mean by that is I didn't want to constantly send items back to consignors because they were not on brand or in good condition. I needed a plan that rewarded bringing in the top brands, penalized high returns due to brand or condition, and had an upside for the salesperson. A contractor came up with the idea of assigning points and rewarding a salesperson based on points, not dollars in. Simply stated, the points system allowed us to calculate a bonus based on the quality of the consignment in, not the quantity. For example, a Rolex generates more dollars in than a pair of Tory Burch flats. And, the Rolex brand is more coveted than most. By matching desirability and dollars, the objective of being a luxury consignment business could be met. Further, it allowed each salesperson to get a salary, and if they achieved a specific number of points per month, we could afford to pay them a bonus. I went to work developing a point system for our Los Angeles team of one.

By the end of September, Dave McClure had come through. 500 Startups had invested—wait for it—$25,000! Woo-hoo. He did it. And then he kept his promise and put in a good word for The RealReal with AngelList. By mid-October, we were on the platform. I sent a note thanking Dave McClure for his pull with AngelList. And before the year ended, we had raised more than $800,000 on AngelList. Did AngelList learn a lesson from this? I don't know, I never heard from them. I hope so. I doubt it. It didn't really matter because that platform delivered for us.

The RealReal was only six months old by the time we rolled into December. I thought we could hit the $10 million goal for the next year. We needed to open up New York City. The AngelList investor infusion had given us the capital to hire someone in this important fashion-oriented city. Our first remote salesperson was killing it in LA. But the local stylist was struggling. Her capacity to contribute to the company was shrinking. She stopped showing up at the office and very rarely brought in product. I had set up a meeting with her in mid-December at the San Rafael office. Our lawyer would be present. I was going to let her go. She didn't show up for the meeting. Only later did we find out that she had moved back to the Chicago area to be with her family.

A member of her family did stop by the office to collect her things but didn't say why she had left, and I didn't feel I had the right to ask. The termination letter on her desk was collected, too.

December 2011 ended, and I felt a mix of hope and discouragement. Seven months into it, the business was working. AngelList was working for us. The stylist's departure was unsettling, but Rati and our LA salesperson were doing well. We had raised enough money to give Rati a raise. The warehouse was filling up. We could have five sales per week. And I was going to find LA person 2.0 in New York City. However, my home life was under stress. I needed to make The RealReal a priority, and it sucked up all of my time. This put considerable stress on my relationship with the U-Haul boyfriend. That was bound to end unless I changed course and did not spend as much time making The RealReal successful. I did not change course, and the relationship did end.

I headed out to New York City in mid-January 2012 to interview candidates. That resulted in a few meetings but not one potential employee. We couldn't afford a recruiter, so we were generating employee leads through friends. I decided to head back to New York in early February.

I had two long days of interviewing people. No one was right for the position. The RealReal kept attracting people who wanted to keep their side hustle or their permanent job and become a The RealReal salesperson on the side. My favorite was the guy who was offered a position on Madonna's tour pretty much as a bag boy, meaning a person in charge of her luggage. Still, he thought he could also work at The RealReal while he was doing that job.

"So, how would you do your job in New York City if you are in London?" I asked him.

"Well, we will get back to New York City."

"But what if you are heading to Milan next?"

"I mean, we will get back to New York City soon."

"I see. And then you'd be willing to go to people's homes, pick up the items, inspect them for condition, and then ship them to California for processing?"

"Is that really the job?"

"Yes, it is."

"Well, I don't want to do all of that all the time."

"Hmm, you probably aren't right for the position."

"Should I contact you when I am back from the tour?"

"Sure."

I never contacted him again. And he was the best of the bunch on that trip. I didn't blame him for trying to have it both ways. But I couldn't build a company with employees who had divergent interests. I needed them to make building The RealReal in New York City their priority. It could not be just a job.

Hiring at a start-up with minimal funding is hard. And it is doubly hard when you are doing something no one has done before because you must sell a dream and get total buy-in without overpromising. Total buy-in and commitment to growing the business are critical for success. Couple that with the job description, and it can be hard to find a great employee. This position involved a lot of schlepping, real physical labor, and it was critical that the salesperson inspect items for condition. This task included sniffing garments to see if they passed the smell test. Nothing says "used clothing" more than strong body odor trapped in the fabric. We had to insist that people deliver the clothing cleaned because the dry-cleaning costs and the liability of

The RealReal handling the dry-cleaning would have seriously hurt the business. And returns, as noted before, are expensive. Sending things back to the consignor because of the condition is expensive for the business and a terrible experience for the consignor. Consequently, if returns were higher than a small percentage, the salesperson received negative points.

I can attest that I have a sensitive nose, a fun fact that I didn't know until I started the business. I can also attest to the fact that Rati doesn't—which means I kept giving her pungent items to smell just for fun, like someone handing you a milk carton and saying, "Smell this. I think the milk has curdled. What do you think?" She only fell for my sniffing requests twice. This didn't stop me from repeatedly asking her. I think my grin and low-volume giggling gave it away every time. It became one of many running jokes we shared as we worked in the warehouse. It was one of my favorites, along with a brainteaser—"How do you think this stain got there?"—as we turned garments inside out for inspection.

Although the sales position had negatives, it also had great positives for the right person. Picking up and discussing people's things was very personal and required building trust. Our LA employee had already developed sweet relationships with her consignors because of the intimate nature of the position. There was an added benefit of being around beautiful luxury items every day. The person also had to be a builder. They had to get excited about creating something that had never been done before. They had to think strategically about how to build the business locally and execute beautifully. They had to be independent and collaborative. They had to be driven to hit their goals. People had to like them. The members of The RealReal sales team were and are the brand. This is all to point out that this job attracted a particular kind of person. Madonna's bag guy clearly was not that person for us. And, after many interviews, I decided New York City could wait until we could raise more capital, open an office there, and pay people a better wage.

It was May 2012, and The RealReal was headed toward a $10 million year. I felt confident enough that I took my home off the market. I knew The RealReal would be a success by then. Now it was time to convince others. It was time to raise venture capital. We were eleven months old and had a repeatable, predictable supply coming from the LA market with our current sales tactics of creating leads for our now two-person team in LA to follow up on. The LA salesperson had done so well, we had been able to hire another one. It felt like we had unlimited demand and not enough product. We needed to expand. It was time for us to get a Series A round of capital.

A venture capital round comes with all kinds of changes in the business. First, a venture capital investor assigns a value to the company. The cash infusion is added to that value, and venture capitalists then own a percentage of the company. It is a simple math equation. For example, if The RealReal was valued at $10 million and I wanted to raise $10 million, and I owned all of the stock prior to the cash infusion, I would now have 50 percent of the stock and so would the investors. The original $10 million plus a cash infusion of $10 million would mean the company was then worth $20 million, and the venture capitalists would have 10 divided by 20, or 50 percent. Ownership dilution is super hard, but it happens. I have worked with entrepreneurs who are obsessed with dilution because they believe they do all of the work and therefore should retain the majority of the company. I am not one of those people. I believe dilution is the lesser of two evils.

Why? If you have ever watched a competitor have enough capital to execute their plan while you are still digging in the dirt and being left behind looking at your potential dilution, you would understand my rationale. Personally, I have not experienced this. I am pragmatic.

However, I have seen companies go into this mode for one reason or another. These companies can become a zombie company. Running a zombie company, a walking dead company, is no fun. Those companies stumble along, put out a press release now and then, and eventually lose so much momentum that they die. They have no growth. If you are not growing, you are dying.

So, it was time to dilute my ownership and that of the other stockholders. The fresh cash would allow me to scale the sales team in key cities and hire a CTO to begin developing our own technology platform. We had already pushed past the capabilities of the technology platform I had chosen to get us started.

I put together a pitch that covered the main points of the business. First, I sized the potential of the business, known as the total available market, or the TAM, and found that number had to be calculated based on the sales of luxury goods over the previous fifteen years. That would later come into question from a prominent venture capitalist who had a "mosaic" of information that indicated my data was incorrect. The next slide talked about The RealReal's competitive differentiation, then the competition, followed by our results to date and use of funds.

I became a pitching machine. We had a venture capitalist firm that came to us via AngelList, e.ventures (now Headline) that had invested approximately $1 million as a seed investor in the spring of 2012. Mathias Schilling, the partner who had sought out The RealReal and then sponsored the investment, was happy to make introductions to other suitable firms. His firm didn't want to lead the deal, but they were committed to adding more capital if I found a lead. I started with his recommendations. He quickly made warm introductions, and meetings were set up relatively easily. Warm introductions make a big difference when getting your foot in the door. That is where they stop. It's not nothing, but it isn't exactly something, either.

The first three meetings were the "not a no" no. Luckily, the "not noes" came within a couple of days after the meeting. This means they were a no, but my representative at the venture fund did not want to use that word. A fast "not no" is better than lingering silence, which could be a yes but probably is a "not no." Those are killers because you can think of all the reasons why the VC will say yes, or at least move you to the next meeting, until they don't do either. The worst investors are the ghosters. Venture capitalists were the OG of ghosting before the word *ghosting* was ever coined. Here is an example of a real no that masquerades as a "not no." The names have been removed to protect those involved.

> *"After digging in and discussing with my team, we've decided not to move forward with your current round. While we're incredibly impressed with what you've built with the company so far and with you as a founder, we need to see more commercial traction to reach conviction here.*
>
> *Again, thanks so much for taking the time to connect, and I'd be happy to stay in touch as you continue building. I'm excited to see how the September program launch pans out, and please feel free to add me to any investor updates you may be sending out. Looking forward to keeping in touch and following your journey!"*

Here is what it says to the founder: We have no faith you can execute, but if you do, we don't want to be left out in the cold, so keep us updated. It is a typical rejection email that manages to be condescending, disrespectful, and completely inauthentic in two paragraphs. Run away from this type of VC or any potential investor who sends these types of notes. They are not worth your time.

I still had two meetings through the Mathias connection. Rati came with me to the one on Sand Hill Road. Sand Hill Road is the road of heartbreak and opportunity for entrepreneurs since nearly every top technology company has received capital from one of the venture firms on Sand Hill. Exiting Highway 280 heading toward downtown Palo Alto, there is signage for over fifty venture capital firms. The signage for each firm is designed and impressive, but the buildings they are attached to are not. Most are somewhat unattractive office complexes. Some look like old roadside motels, California style. The exteriors don't even hint at the monumental wealth created within the walls for the entrepreneurs and the partners. Once you walk into the office, you understand clearly that these people are wealthy and successful. The interiors are designed to showcase the firm, usually by showing off their remarkable art collection accented by designer chairs, plush rugs, and impressive chandeliers. Oddly, very few showcase the very reason for their wealth: the entrepreneurs and companies they have funded. There is a subtle indication that the partner you are about to meet is the reason any business is successful because this guy (mostly men) knows how to pick the winners.

Luckily for Rati, her first Sand Hill Road meeting was one of the most entertaining meetings I have had. We walked into a stunning lobby done in soft beiges with marble floors and expensive art on the walls. The receptionist was an attractive twenty-something woman in a tight dress with a lot of cleavage—really more of a Los Angeles look than an understated Palo Alto look. She escorted us into the conference room and gave us the Wi-Fi password so we could present our PowerPoint. I handed her a coupon to try The RealReal. Ever the promoter, I gave those discount coupons out to every woman I met.

The venture capitalist came in and asked us not to present, just talk him through the business. Okay, it was going to be a dialogue.

Sometimes it is easier to have a conversation, but mostly it is better to walk people through a presentation so you don't miss key points. I started discussing the luxury market, how large the primary market was, how the goods piled up in people's closets, and how the only ways to dispose of them was to donate them, drop them off at the corner consignment store, or sell them on eBay. I explained that eBay was not a luxury platform and that selling on eBay was entirely too hard and time consuming. I gave him the derived TAM number and the assumptions I used to derive that number. Last, I talked about how The RealReal solved real problems.

He just listened. Didn't seem to be engaged. And he hadn't yet asked a question. Still, I kept talking, but at some point, I realized that I should have checked out his background before I walked into the meeting. That is a critical step everyone should do, and yet I had not done it. Understanding the investor's background gives a good understanding of their perspective. There was a high probability he had worked at eBay (as many venture capitalists had done) in some capacity and had a hard time envisioning The RealReal's potential. We had already been told by another venture capitalist who was an ex-eBayer that eBay was a fine solution and The RealReal was not any different, just a smaller market potential.

I took a breath and asked if he had any questions. He put his foot on the table and said, "See this shoe?"

I didn't respond. His foot had an ugly muddy brown shoe on it. He continued, "I have had these shoes for five years. What do you think of that?"

"I don't think you are my customer."

He didn't crack a smile. The meeting was clearly over. We never heard from him, although Mathias did. The firm gave us a firm "no." Unbeknownst to Mathias and me, this firm had a company on its books that was considering pivoting away from a baby-clothes-sharing site to a low-end resale marketplace. That firm was called ThredUp. ThredUp did eventually pivot to the resale marketplace. Like The RealReal, ThredUp did all of the work for the consignor, except it didn't have a sales force and its average selling price was $39, while The RealReal's average selling price at the time was $495.

The best venture capital meetings give you some insight that you may have missed or an idea of forthcoming challenges. This meeting was just odd and unproductive. I had thought it might be weird for a different reason. I knew about some shenanigans concerning a different partner in the firm, and he knew that I knew. Did that enter into their consideration? I'll never know for sure. But even if it was a minor factor, I kind of knew it had the possibility to sway the deal. Venture capitalists have different ways of greenlighting a deal—some require all partners to agree on the deal, some do not.

We had one more Mathias warm introduction, with Greycroft, a venture firm based in Los Angeles and New York City. Rati and I met with Dana Settle, one of the founding partners. She loved the idea and was impressed with the vision and the progress we had made. All she had to do was convince her partners. She asked for any data we had. She had already heard of The RealReal and decided to try it. This was progress. Not a yes, but real progress.

While Greycroft was working its process, I was meeting with a couple more early stage venture capital women. One was really interested in what we were doing. We met in a coffee shop on Fillmore Street in San Francisco and had a long conversation. I walked her through my pitch, then she asked for the numbers and the PowerPoint presentation. This was showing promise. Women venture capitalists seemed to get what we were doing. They shopped. They bought expensive things. They had no easy way to monetize their purchases when they stopped using them. This woman was extremely interested in The RealReal's business proposition, and she usually coinvested with a larger firm back east. Her firm was too small to be the lead—the investor who sets the price and the terms for the round—but the other firm could.

Our San Rafael facility was a crazy, chaotic, glorious mess. If VCs saw the momentum and experienced the energy, they would be more inspired when they presented the deal to their partners. But none seemed interested in venturing north to the San Rafael Canal district to visit the worldwide headquarters of The RealReal. None except Mathias Schilling. Mathias came and spent time with us. He sat between people authenticating pieces, Container Store plastic shoeboxes filled with designer handbags, and shoes piled so high they reached the ceiling and tilted like the Leaning Tower of Pisa from the heat and lack of structure around them. He asked a lot of questions as I fretted about the plastic containers falling on his head.

By the time Mathias made his visit to The RealReal, we had two potential investors evaluating the deal, Dana Settle and the coffee shop VC, who was about to show her real colors. I really thought both were moving in the right direction. Of the two, only Dana Settle could lead the deal, so if she did not invest, I would be back to square one. With that in mind, I went in search of a new lead.

I reached out to one of the senior partners at Canaan Partners, Eric Young. I had met him years before and found him to be super smart and curious. He set up a meeting quickly and asked one of his partners, Maha Ibrahim, to join the meeting. They listened to the entire pitch. Eric was highly skeptical that our salespeople would be allowed into people's homes. He stated emphatically that his wife would never let that happen.

"We were in your home yesterday picking up consignment," I said without blinking. He about fell over.

Maha quickly said, "I love this business. I need to see your numbers. This is exciting. We have our partners' meeting on Monday. Can you present then?"

"We'd love to."

I was delighted. Shortly after we presented, we had a lead investor in Canaan.

Once I knew we had a lead investor, I placed a call to Mathias. Mathias knew Maha, liked her, and was excited. He was also committed to the round. We had nearly $8 million with just these two investors.

Dana of Greycroft asked us to keep the round open for her and said she needed a bit more time. The men in the firm didn't understand the concept. She said she would keep working them.

I emailed the Fillmore Street coffee shop venture capitalist to let her know that we had a term sheet coming and asked her if she was interested in participating in the round.

I didn't hear back from her. Our $10 million Series A round had Canaan as the lead and e.ventures and Greycroft rounding out the deal. A day later, another resale business focused on the luxury space announced funding. Threadflip, a luxury fashion site, announced it had received $10 million in funding from, among others, the coffee shop venture capitalist. It didn't take a genius to realize she had asked for my numbers and presentation as part of her due diligence for the company she had decided to invest in.

Now, she didn't *have* to tell me that she was in the latter stages of making an investment in a fashion resale company that could be considered a competitor. She had no legal requirement to do so. But ethically and as a good person who has a long-term perspective, she should have. Most venture capitalists would have. In Indiana, we would have called her move sleazy. If she had been honest with me, I would not have shown her my numbers and the pitch.

Here's an interesting dynamic that happens repeatedly in new business formation. When I started The RealReal, unbeknownst to me, several other resale sites were starting up. Resale was apparently in the zeitgeist. If you follow technology, this happens repeatedly. It is like we are accessing the same invisible channel. For The RealReal, I needed to understand the other players getting funded in the fashion or resale space, as I would be asked about them all the time.

There was one company that could have been a real competitor, Threadflip. However, in observing the company, the founder appeared to be overly focused on the technology, not the supply. The RealReal was focusing on supply, not technology. As I mentioned, we recognized early on that we were a technology-enabled business, not a technology business. Without the ability to source supply—meaning fashion in The RealReal's case—a resale marketplace does not exist. Buyers rely on supply. Threadflip apparently thought it was a technology company. It never made it past Series B funding. Focusing on the wrong priority is a common mistake first-time entrepreneurs make. You must apply your capital to the single most important lever in the business and make choices to live with a less-than-ideal situation or solution in other areas of the business. Capital prioritization is most likely the difference between succeeding and failing. This isn't that different in larger companies, but the rigor needed in a start-up is different. When you are starting a business, you are always on the thin edge of a knife. A few false moves, and it gets ugly.

I constantly evaluate business-to-consumer businesses and project their success or where they will hit the wall. As a consummate armchair entrepreneur quarterback, I have been right more times than wrong. My timing has been off, though. Timing is the toughest thing to predict. The best example is Pets.com. Nearly twenty years after Pets .com was shuttered, Chewy.com is flourishing. This is good practice for any entrepreneur. You can always learn from other businesses, even from afar, especially if you understand their sector or their customer focus. Assess a company's product offering—is it unique? Its pricing model—is it competitive? Its competitive barriers to entry—who else can replicate the company? If you are really interested, buy the company's product, and see if it delivers on the value proposition. Study its ad spend and marketing message—does it map to the products the company sells? Ask yourself whether you would become a repeat customer here or a one-and-done customer. Understand its competitive set—why is this company different? Evaluate its timing, which is sometimes hard to understand in real time and best observed in the rearview mirror. Bad timing can be the sole determinant of success.

Chapter 4

Show Me the Money

I raised the capital in 2012 midyear, and it was clear that business would exceed $10 million that year. We had completed our first full year in business and had achieved $10 million a year from June 2011 to June 2012. In fact, the demand never flagged. If we had the product in the warehouse, we would sell it quickly, with all products gone in ninety days. We priced the product to move within a ninety-day window at an optimal price, not necessarily the highest price. The Real-Real was and is in the selling business, not the warehousing business. We needed more infrastructure to support the business.

The first step in this process was building out the team. The business was heading toward $20 million, and we needed to up our game on talent. Rati and I had been doing pretty much everything with a few hourly employees for more than a year. The new funding allowed us to hire some professional people to help drive and support the growth. And then we hired Maria Castro. Maria was our head of shipping and customer service. We hired her despite her total lack of experience in those areas. And she was good at both. Maria kind of appeared out of nowhere. We were not advertising for a new hire, but we certainly needed people.

She had been a customer of The RealReal since 2011, our founding year. One day she placed an order for a handbag and sent a note to customer service, asking if she could pick up her order. Customer service was my job at the time, so I responded to her, "Sure, you can come to our office and pick up your order." I included our address in the order.

Then I turned to Rati: "A customer wants to come *here* and pick up her order. I'll meet her at the front door." We both turned a little white. The San Rafael office was not a place for customer drop-ins. We still had the black garbage bags taped over the windows and the crunchy brown carpet. And we had product everywhere. There were so many rolling racks and plastic containers full of shoes and handbags stacked everywhere, it barely left a way to move between areas. It was a controlled mess.

Early the next day, Maria knocked at the door. I stepped outside with her order in hand and thanked her for placing the order and asked her how she heard about the company. As I was turning around to go back inside, she asked if she could use our restroom. Hard to refuse, I let her in and guided her through the mess. As she crunched across the floor and wove her way to the photography area and the restroom, I was dying to get a look at her face. I am sure she could not believe this. Any dreams had to have been shattered. I went back to my desk and continued to answer customer service questions. She reappeared, sat down next to me, and said, "I want to work here." She handed me her resume. I looked at it and was immediately struck by the length of employment at her current company. She had been there eleven years and held a management position in training.

"Why would you leave your current position?"

Maria leaned in and said, "I want to work in fashion."

"We don't have any openings, but we do need help in customer service and operations."

"I'm willing to do anything." I could tell from her face that she was sincere.

"We are a start-up; it's risky."

"I can see that. I'd like to work here."

"I'll get back to you tomorrow. Can I reach you at the number on your resume?" Maria said yes and stood up. I helped her maneuver toward the door.

I turned to Rati, "Someone who has a real job wants to work here. We need help. I can only afford to offer her $45,000 to run customer service and operations. I'm going to call her tomorrow and offer her that position."

"She'll never take it," Rati said. "I bet she is making $20,000 to $35,000 more than that right now."

"You are working here for that amount, and have you looked at your hourly wage? It's probably $2.50 an hour."

"That's different," Rati said.

Maria was making a lot more in her current job. Still, she took the job at The RealReal as offered and started each day with infectious goodwill and positivity. She was living the dream.

The next step: more space. I found a place at the ICB Building at Gate 5 Road in Sausalito. Close to the Bay and a few yacht harbors, the ICB is an old military building converted to artist studios and some warehouse/commerce space. Moving there enabled us to quadruple our warehouse capacity. We had an office space in a loft above the warehouse.

The new building and fresh capital allowed us a little breathing room. I hired a full-time accountant, a VP of marketing, and a few others right away. I started interviewing for a CFO.

Just moving into a bigger space by the water gave a new energy to the business. You could smell the Bay, not bacon, from the office. There were two dining options within a five-minute walk. Across the street was the Seahorse restaurant, with its driftwood art and macramé plant holder decor that hadn't been updated since the 1970s. And Fish restaurant, a local Sausalito favorite, was just a few hundred steps away. Both were major upgrades from the sandwich shop.

The drawbacks of the ICB Building didn't immediately present themselves. When the first king tide happened, it became clear. Car alarms went off and a couple of cars started floating around, bumping into other cars. The parking lot facing the bay side had significant flooding. Once we saw the lot start to fill with water, we all raced out to move our cars, but soon found out that parking on the other side of the building had other challenges. Racoons. A pack of them had settled under the building by the refuse bins. You were guaranteed to be chased by one or two of them all the way to your car if you left through the back door, which of course, you had to do during high tides.

And then there were our neighbors, the artists. Turns out they weren't that pleased that art now had commerce next to it. This was not peanut butter and chocolate. There was one woman directly above us who used to start loudly pounding on her floor—our ceiling—around 3 p.m. each day. I went upstairs to see if I could find out who was so aggravated with us, but all the doors to the studios were closed. This went on for months. One day, she got so exasperated she came down to confront us.

I answered the door, and she screamed at me, "I create art all day. What do you create?"

"I create jobs. Want to look around? We are hiring."

She didn't want a job, but she did want to look around, and the tension was eased a bit.

By the fall, the business was accelerating even faster. We were again on a run rate that was more than doubling the business. We needed more people and better processes. I was reluctant to hire more people because the initial raise of $10 million was not lasting that long. We still hadn't opened up New York City. But unless we hired more people, especially in key markets, to bring in product, we could not grow. We needed to raise another round of fresh capital in the late fall or early the next year.

Entrepreneurs live by the phrase "always be selling." I was at the beginning of that cycle. Turns out, for the next ten years I was always selling because I was always raising money. I raised capital every six to nine months. And every step of the way it was fun and challenging and maddening.

I needed to raise more capital in 2013, so I registered The RealReal in a Fashion Tech event held on a stage in New York City in October. Daymond John, entrepreneur and regular "shark" investor on *Shark Tank*, was the master of ceremonies. The format was simple. Entrepreneurs would pitch their business to a team of venture capitalist judges, who would then give them feedback. The arena-style venue held about two thousand people, but only the judges could ask questions.

I sat in the wings waiting for my time. An entrepreneur pitching her motorcycle jackets was on stage. There were three judges, two men and the coffee shop VC, the woman who had invested in The Real-Real's competitor and had The RealReal's confidential information.

This was the first time I had presented in public since the downfall of Pets.com. Once upon a time, I had been a very good public speaker. I always felt that I knew my subject better than anyone else, so why be nervous? I prided myself on being able to explain businesses clearly to anyone, including sophisticated investors and my neighbors, who were far removed from being professional investors.

But that was then. I now found myself in a full panic attack. Kind of a PTSD reaction. I felt like I was reliving the terrible slaughtering I had taken in the press post-Pets.com. It felt like what I thought a stroke or a heart attack might feel like. My heart was racing. I could barely breathe. I walked away from the curtain and started taking deep breaths. I shut my eyes and sat down. I drank a sip of water and felt a tingling sensation run down my back. My name was called. I had to go on stage.

As I slowly walked onto the stage, I knew I had to steady my voice. And I needed to focus my eyes. I did not want to look at the massive audience. Then I saw the competitor investor, and she smiled at me like we were besties. What a gift that was. Seeing her broke my panic. Panic was replaced with a bit of anger and a lot of determination. I was still aghast at her actions. She wasn't going to get the best of me.

I presented The RealReal's business without hesitation and with great fluidity. I felt my old self materialize and found my rhythm. I answered the judges' questions succinctly. As I was leaving the stage, Daymond John was walking onto stage. He started questioning the validity of my business, talking about how he could buy a Louis Vuitton bag on every corner in New York City, and asking why anyone would want to use The RealReal. The crowd laughed a little.

Ten minutes earlier, his comments would have panicked me. Now, I looked at his back from the side of the stage and thought, "Go back to the T-shirt business, Daymond."

The next day, I flew back to our normal day-to-day controlled chaos at work. The business was more than doubling. We still were all doing everything, despite adding staff.

I had one more monumental trip back to New York City in November of that year. Dana Settle, our investor from Greycroft, had asked me to come to their holiday party, held at a swanky venue in the Flatiron

District. I was still working seven days a week and was tired, and I'm just not that social, but I felt like I had to do it. Greycroft, along with Canaan and e.ventures, had taken a chance on me and the business. The least I could do was thank them in person and let them know that I would work hard to give them a great return on their capital.

Within minutes of walking into the event, I saw Alan Patricof, one of the founding partners of Greycroft. I walked up with an extended hand, introduced myself, and started my thank-you speech. He stopped me short.

"I don't like your business. I didn't want to invest," he said. "I only agreed because I am trying to support my partners."

I took a step back and just stood there. He stood there, too. Then I asked him where the bar was, followed his directions, had a drink, went back to the hotel room, and booked an earlier flight to San Francisco the next day. As the saying goes . . . with friends like these. I had their money, so I had to shrug off his comments and move on. I had a lot of work in front of me. It didn't matter what he said. Results mattered.

The year ended with revenue numbers showing we were more than doubling. The next year could be well over $40 million in top-line revenue if we continued at this pace. The business was on fire. I would need to raise more money in the first quarter of 2013. It appeared we had unlimited demand. We did not have unlimited supply. We needed to add more people in key cities to pick up supply. And we needed more marketing dollars to support more lead generation to support more people in the field. And, if that worked, and I kind of knew it would, we would need more people to authenticate, to take photos, to pick, pack, and ship.

I estimated that we had only barely scratched the surface of success. Maybe we had cornered .0001 percent of the market. If we didn't grow the supply, we would start shrinking. Once I had secured the capital, we would have to move again. We were slowly taking over the large sections of the ICB Building. Moving was so disruptive. We lost two to three days of work and employees with each move. The deposit money for the new space and the increased rent were always a consideration, too. I hated paying rent and tying up our capital in a landlord deposit. I might be able to push the move until the end of 2013, early 2014. Maybe.

Chapter 5

If You Aren't Growing, You Are Dying

We entered 2013 needing to raise more capital, as predicted. We had ended 2012 at $20 million top-line revenue and looked like we were going to double again. But the first priority going into the new year was hiring the right person to run New York City. And we had a great candidate in the funnel, Rachel Vaisman, an executive at Dior on maternity leave who wanted a new position that didn't require as much travel to France. An offer was made, and she took the position. She would oversee setting up our first office and distribution center in New York City and run sales. But first she had to find the office, create a mini operations center, hire salespeople, take out the trash, and turn out the lights. Basically, do it all. With Bay Area staff support.

We found a space on West 36th Street on the third floor. There was expansion space in the building, and it had a good, operating freight elevator. It wasn't a union building, which kept the costs down, but it did have its quirks, which would reveal themselves over time. Specifically, a very tan guy with an open shirt and lots of gold jewelry would show up regularly at our office and ask us to sign another waste management contract. He had a key to the space. It wasn't unusual for him to just be there when people returned from lunch. Rachel was tough, but this guy was unnerving. Complaining to the building management did not solve the problem. Signing his contract would have, and we were about to do this when the building was raided and the building manager was arrested for selling drugs. The tan guy never showed up after that.

The space needed painting, air conditioning, and new doors and lighting. Rachel hired a project manager and started on all of it.

These tenant improvements and another coinciding event created a rather infamous but short-lived moment at The RealReal—naked day.

The merchandising team received photos of a celebrity for her celebrity sale on the site. The only problem with the photos was that she did not have clothes on. She had strategically placed fur or other items on her body. Within minutes of someone receiving those completely inappropriate but widely shared photos, and completely coincidentally, a technician testing the office's new surveillance cameras happened upon a spectacular scene. Five rather hefty men painting the walls and installing the security door were all working naked. Rachel explained later that day that the workers didn't like to sweat in their clothes. So, every day before they left the office, they cleaned up in the bathroom and put their clothes back on. During construction, we temporarily shut down the cameras. No more naked workmen. I wish I could say the same for celebrity pictures—those continued to occasionally flow in.

New York City was open for business now. And the product was flowing in. I dusted off my investor pitch and started knocking on doors again.

After extensive due diligence, Interwest Capital invested, and Keval Desai joined the board. He added a new element to the board of directors. He was an operator and engineer by training and had spent most of his working days at Google. This gave him a completely different perspective from the other investors who had built their careers in the venture capital industry.

The year 2013 ended with the company at $50 million in top-line revenue. We exited that year with a run rate that implied we would double again, and we had moved to a warehouse on Oakdale Avenue in San Francisco. The place used to be a pie factory—the kind sold at gas stations in a wrapper like a candy bar. It had over 30,000 square feet of warehouse space with office space in the loft above the warehouse, similar to the ICB Building. We had a working kitchen, some beautiful brickwork inside the pie-cooling area, and most important, some breathing room for our continuous expansion.

The executive team had expanded in 2013, too. We had added a new CFO and an ex-eBay executive. We were slowly adding structure to our budgeting process and forecasts. We had the beginning of a real finance department.

The year 2014 brought more excitement, including developing a relationship with Neiman Marcus and Saks Fifth Avenue, bringing in a new investor, and taking many meetings with an infamous Hollywood agent turned venture capitalist who requested that I meet with him. And the year brought more growth.

I had been meeting with executives from both Neiman Marcus and Saks Fifth Avenue after we had our first funding. The pitch was simple: The RealReal will help your clients clean out their closets and buy more of your product for their empty closets. Clients consigning with The RealReal will receive Neiman Marcus or Saks gift cards, so the money your clients make will come back to you. We are willing to incentivize your sales team for recommending The RealReal. All you have to do is conduct internal sales training on our service, promote it to your clients in store, and then sit back and capture the sale when your customers redeem the cards. At that time, The RealReal was paying consignors at the rate of $30 million a year, and the business was still doubling.

Neiman Marcus agreed first. The project required some technical development on both sides and event coordination. One of our top executives, Allison Sommer, was heading the project. We launched across all Neiman Marcus stores.

Saks was more hesitant but ultimately didn't want to be left out in the cold. It wanted to roll out the program with its special Saks Club members and offer it as a perk both for the company's elite sales team that serviced these buyers and the members. Although that didn't make sense to us, we were eager to get our foot in the door, and so we said yes.

The program was going very well. The first few months, we distributed over $40,000 worth of gift cards to Neiman Marcus customers. Saks was a small fraction of that amount, but it was a start. The next month even more Neiman Marcus and Saks people joined the program and The RealReal had a desk at high-volume Neiman Marcus stores. The third month saw even greater growth. We were meeting new clients and turning them into new RealReal consignors at a good, cost-effective clip.

It was—as corny salespeople say—a win, win, win. Until it wasn't. Neiman Marcus was the first to schedule a call.

"Chanel wants you to stop picking up their pieces from Neiman Marcus customers. If you do not do this, we will have to end the relationship," Allison told me.

I then repeated what she said, only with a question mark at the end: "Chanel wants us to stop picking up Chanel pieces? Or Neiman Marcus will end the relationship with us?"

Yes and yes.

I took a deep breath. Even if we wanted to go along with Chanel's request, how would we differentiate a Neiman Marcus customer from other customers? The answer is we could not, and our guess was that there already was a high overlap between Neiman Marcus customers and The RealReal customers. This felt like a blatant attempt from Chanel to restrict our ability to conduct business.

"Well, we will have to wind down the relationship then."

It appeared that Chanel had been targeting The RealReal for a while. According to our advertising executives at the *New York Times* and *Women's Wear Daily*, Chanel had blocked our ads from running in those publications. It had also blocked our ads when we tried to run in a couple of women's magazines.

The Saks call came a week later. A young, rather off-putting snippy woman set up the meeting. She was not part of the executive team we had been dealing with during the negotiations. Her speech to us went something like "The partnership we have with you isn't working. We want to terminate it immediately."

"I see. This is because of Chanel, isn't it?" I responded.

"No, it's not."

"Well, we had a similar conversation with Neiman Marcus, and they were forthcoming about Chanel demanding that we cease picking up Chanel items from Neiman Marcus customers," I said calmly.

"We need to terminate the relationship immediately; it is not working." Clearly, she had her script, and she was sticking to it.

And so, thanks to Chanel, our strategic partnerships came to an immediate end. These events are also cited in allegations in a Chanel, Inc. v. The RealReal, Inc. lawsuit that is pending as of this publication date.

I believe that Chanel has the philosophy that someone who purchases one of its products has no right to resell it. At one point, it included a card in its handbags that stated something like this. So, in effect, a consumer can never recover anything from their original purchase. I am not sure this is even legally enforceable. Ferrari also provides significant limits on its auto sales, including that the buyer cannot sell the car during the first year of ownership. Chanel appeared to be trying to emulate Ferrari.

Chanel couldn't stop our growth or our ability to pick up Chanel. The short-lived relationships we had with these retailers, Neiman Marcus in particular, had increased our awareness with our target audience. And Chanel products rolled through The RealReal doors every hour. Significant quantities came in and sold quickly at a nice discount.

The second big thing that happened that year was we added a new investor to our capitalization table. This new investor also expanded our horizons in ways the others did not. After a long process, we had a good term sheet from a venture capital firm called Double Bottom Line (DBL). The firm's mission was to invest in companies that were good for the planet and make money at the same time. DBL was one of the first investors in Tesla when other venture capitalists declined to invest in the deal. The firm seemed like a great fit for The RealReal, but one of the partners had extreme discomfort with our focus on the luxury market.

She eventually extended an invitation to me to join her on a panel the Ellen MacArthur Foundation was sponsoring in San Francisco. This foundation was a thought leader in how manufacturing could be transformed to become more circular. It was also instrumental in raising awareness of the damage that plastics are doing to the environment. It hadn't yet focused on the impact of fashion in landfills or the danger of the slow breakdown and leaching of plastics found in fabrics. I had not heard the term *circular economy* until that conference. It perfectly described what The RealReal was doing.

After the panel, I cornered the foundation's representatives to set up a meeting and explore how we could work together. I needed to raise their awareness about the impact of fashion on the environment. They had the resources to further the research on the impact of discarded fashion items. They had already quantified a very descriptive data point, specifically, one truckload of fashion goes into a landfill every six seconds worldwide. They also demonstrated the ability to impact laws at the EU level.

This meeting was the beginning of collaboration and information sharing that went on for years. A few months after this meeting, The RealReal would take the next step by hiring environmental scientists to quantify the positive impact of recirculating clothing instead of buying new. Those numbers proved to be powerful reinforcers of our environmental message. The year-end summary of individual carbon savings due to consigning or buying resale had the added benefit of making our customers feel good about participating in an activity that was good for the planet.

At some point, we decided to add the positive environmental impact of recirculating goods to our marketing approach. It was already part of the company's mission statement, but we had been intentionally quiet about it to our customer base, both consignors and consumers. That was by design.

When marketing a business or new product, it is best to have one clear message that is salient to the consumer and encourages them to act. This is especially true when you have a new type of business that disrupts the current market and doesn't have a clear precedent. Although consignment stores have been around a long time, The Real-Real needed to stay focused on supply and demand and the bottom line. It was a bonus that our business was good for the world. And it made me feel as though I was making a difference.

The RealReal wanted to understand what motivated our customers to shop and consign there, so we distributed regular surveys. Environmental factors didn't make the top ten list for the first three years. By the fourth year, this motivation had made it into the top five reasons for shopping and consigning at The RealReal. Yet that had not been part of our messaging. A further look at the data showed it was the younger millennials in our customer base who instinctively knew this was the right thing to do for the planet. Once we picked up that signal, we knew we could introduce it to the base by marketing it everywhere.

Now, just a little bit about that infamous Hollywood person. He knew one of our investors and asked to meet with me. Of course, I said yes. There isn't any harm in a meeting. One meeting turned into a meeting every other week at his request for eight weeks. The first day he showed up, I had a rescue dog with me that shed badly. I was covered in dog hairs. He gave me a look up and down that signaled complete disapproval. I thought that was funny and asked him if he wanted to hold the dog. He said no and became more annoyed. He kind of bounced in his seat when he was annoyed.

The meetings were always coded. I would ask direct questions, and he wouldn't answer anything directly. The only direct things he said to me was that The RealReal was going to be too big, I couldn't run it by myself, and I had hired too many young women. His rationale for the latter statement is that they would all leave to marry someone and have babies. He never invested, and I certainly was not stepping aside to have him help me run the company. After the fourth meeting, he drifted away.

Chapter 6

You Win Some . . .

Here's what happened once we secured financing to our top-line revenue for the next four years.

2012, June: $10 million in revenue

2013, End of Year: Revenue doubled

2014, End of Year: Revenue more than doubled

2015, End of Year: Revenue doubled

2016, End of Year: Revenue more than doubled

We were hiring key people for key positions as fast as we could. We had done this every year since The RealReal's formation, but going from $10 million to $20 million was a lot easier than going from $50 million to $100 million, let alone more than doubling after that. When a business is doubling, hiring the right people is the difference between executing brilliantly and the wheels potentially coming off the wagon.

Hiring is always hard, especially in today's world. Former managers often do not give authentic references because of the threat of being sued by former employees. Back-channel conversations with those who have worked with or for the person happen regularly. But who knows if those people giving the reference have an axe to grind, have ever seen a growth company, or are even good at their jobs?

Then there is the unique Silicon Valley problem. Many in the Valley have made money because they were on a rocket ship and they held on. They may or may not have ever owned a project. They may or may not have been accountable for an area and have been held to objectives. They may or may not have deep analytical skills. They may spin out of their current positions because they are finally held to results. Those people are the silent killers in start-ups. You have to fire them quickly before they metastasize and negatively impact the company. Silicon Valley is speckled with employees who were there for the ride but didn't really do anything personally to contribute to the growth of a company or didn't want to be accountable. And if they were at a start-up that didn't go anywhere—and most don't—they never experienced a company in growth mode. Their resume tends to have one- to two-year stints at various companies and most can continue to sell themselves into the next start-up.

Then there are the personal brand builders, blooming from a new influencer era of narcissistic employees who think the company is all about how they look to others in the company, not what they do and the results they achieve. These people are a nasty problem because they can be quite charismatic, and people are attracted to this energy. But they are not right for a start-up. Start-ups are a team sport. Technology start-ups are highly collaborative, and each functional area is interdependent on the other functional areas to create a great product. No one is the star. The business isn't personal. While this statement is true in

any company, a growth company has its own challenges with employees who give an inordinate amount of time to help the company grow
and yet still may need to be let go because they can't keep up with the
pace or the demands. They feel like they have made great personal
sacrifices joining a high-growth company. And they have. There is no
doubt about that. But that doesn't mean they get to stay in their position if they are not performing.

A growth business with a collaborative process requires people to own their part of the process and the results, and they need
to be ready to iterate quickly when things go wrong. It requires agile
problem-solving based on data. It requires a mindset of doing your
best and then making quick changes when whatever you thought was
working doesn't work. So, if a company hires a few or even one personal brand builder in a prominent position, that person may be more
inclined to cover up their mistakes and to shine on other executives.
This person may even use a bad interpretation of data to support their
greatness. That works if they are great and are achieving results. But
mostly personal brand builders don't achieve great results because it
requires failing—failing within a group and then owning it and fixing
it. Silicon Valley is full of personal brand builders.

On the positive side, a great employee deeply rooted in the Silicon
Valley way of doing and thinking can creatively move mountains in
a start-up. They are always problem-solving. They recognize it's not
about them. They aren't afraid of breaking the mold or precedents or
how things should be done. They see things differently and get excited
by the creative collaborative process. They love getting stuff done. They
love owning things. They love working with smart people. Creating a
new business or a new project is fun. They are grounded in data and
creativity. They are not hierarchical; they are collaborative. They can
scale because they are curious and love to solve all types of problems,

and they understand what moves the needle. That is where those people focus. Those people are gold. They make everyone around them better.

Then there are employees who come from a corporate environment. Corporate employees tend to have a hard adjustment to a Silicon Valley start-up environment. They have typically come from a hierarchical environment. Their thinking or their processes tend toward rigidity, especially if they come from a larger corporation. Corporate employees don't invent new companies; they keep the one they are in from coming off the rails. They tend to be more political, especially in a low-growth business that has low individual accountability. They see it as the only way to get promoted or receive a better assignment or a higher salary. They can get great at shining up and still get promoted even when they don't add to the business at all. They tend to like security and comfort. Even if the company is a technology company, the larger that company gets, the more they attract these people. People tend to hire people like them. So, their new hires learn to suck up hard because that is how their boss got their power and energy and the new hires want to succeed, too. These people tend to wash out quickly in a start-up. Sucking up works at start-ups. Because most founders are pretty beaten down by trying to launch a business and get funding, they are somewhat more vulnerable to anyone saying nice things to them. That is, until they aren't. Because results matter at start-ups, and you can't hide for long.

I recognize that these are all broad generalizations. There are always exceptions. We hired a couple of excellent exceptions. Rachel Vaisman is one.

The RealReal also hired many of the wrong people. And some of them got to stay too long at the party because there was never a good time to let them go—at least that was the story I told myself.

I can say emphatically that it is the wrong decision to keep a non-performing employee on your team. I have been guilty of doing that. But most of the time I wasn't.

By 2015, the business was getting more complex. We needed more talent in our engineering department, we needed more talent in our operations department, and we needed more talent in our sales leadership. The greatest pain points were engineering and operations. Our CTO had left early in our transition away from our starter technology, the platform we had licensed at the beginning. His successor was a guy who could get quite passionate about the work and his role in the company. He hired an exceptional engineer, Fredrik Björk. Fredrik had been an entrepreneur and sold his company to Second Life, a virtual world that is inhabited by virtual people. He knew how to get things done quickly. He was also very technical and could hire good technical talent.

The operations part of the business was harder. We were growing out of our space in New York City and needed to find a large warehouse that was easily commutable from Midtown. Even our new space in Oakdale looked like it wouldn't last long. I figured in a few months we would have to move the warehouse portion again to a much bigger space. I needed someone I could trust to make the right decisions in the operations space. I called up an old friend and colleague, Chris Deyo, to help us out. Eventually he would be known as Chris dot Deyo. After some arm twisting and a solid contract negotiation, Chris joined The RealReal to head up operations.

As we were managing to manage our growth in 2015, two of my most important personal relationships were in tatters. One of those relationships was with the man I was living with, also known as the U-Haul boyfriend. The other one was with a very old, dear friend.

I couldn't have predicted the other relationship that broke. He was one of my best friends, and we had known each other when we were teenagers. We studied together at Purdue. He was a senior vice president at a large advertising agency in Chicago and was on disability due to an autoimmune disease when I founded The RealReal. The newer drugs had started to work for him, but he still needed to take various drugs for various conditions. Yet, despite having only a few good hours a day, he wanted to help with the office design in our Oakdale place. I was thrilled. His creative eye was undeniable. Plus, it would be fun to have him stay with me.

My friend visited at a time when my relationship with my partner was at its breaking point. My partner moved out. My friend stayed for a while. One night, I called my friend from the office. We had an issue in our operations department, and I was going to miss our dinner. I just couldn't make it. He was already at the restaurant. I apologized profusely and told him I would meet him at my house.

I came home to a man raging at me, my closest friend. I wasn't sure what to do about it. It was not a behavior I had seen in him before. At some point, I felt physically threatened. I was visibly shaken. We both went to our bedrooms. We said very little to each other for the balance of his stay. After he moved out, I never talked to him again. We did text back and forth, but his texts didn't make sense. I kept thinking it was the drug cocktail he was on. Something had snapped in him, and I knew it wasn't about me. I couldn't keep texting him back, and slowly he stopped texting me. Two friends were gone. One of them I missed profoundly. Neither did I want back in my life.

Start-ups can take a toll on relationships. I had changed. I was preoccupied. I was having the time of my life, and I was stressed all the time. I was happy stressed. I spent almost all my waking hours thinking about The RealReal. I didn't take a work-free vacation. My sleep was always disrupted. I was never fully present in a conversation unless it was about The RealReal. Relationships got redefined. Some got broken. Was it worth it? For me, it was, without a doubt. Most things and many people get less time and are less of a priority when you start a company. This is the trade-off an entrepreneur must be aware of and willing to make. You won't fully understand the consequences of your decision to start a business until you are well into it. And it is harder for women with living parents, children—anyone who is dependent on you emotionally and/or financially. It is important to be aligned with your priorities.

Meanwhile, as my personal relationships were faltering, in 2015 some amazing things were happening with The RealReal. Recognition was coming our way. The first one was great for the company, the second one was great for me personally.

The company was included in the BoF 500, the Business of Fashion's five hundred people and companies deemed significantly important in the fashion industry. An announcement went out to the entire company, and then we had a team meeting. Everyone was thrilled. Who knew that anyone—besides Chanel—even knew what we were doing? It was a major energy boost to the entire company. I made plans to attend the BoF celebration in London. Business of Fashion was, at the time, a relatively new fashion publication founded by Imran Amed aiming to fill the void that *Women's Wear Daily* left, mostly an analytical approach to reporting on the fashion industry.

The event in London was a buzzy night full of fashion models who were usually in luxury ads and whom I mostly recognized but didn't know their names. I wore a long black Alexander McQueen dress that wasn't trendy, but I felt good in it. After a quick selfie with Imran, I found my seat. I was at the technology table. On my left was a UK fashion company founder who had an odd, hard-to-place accent. On my right was the founder of Farfetch, José Neves, and a few seats down from me was the legendary Julie Gilhart.

Julie had been the senior vice president and fashion director of Barneys New York for more than eighteen years. She had been responsible for bringing new designers, including Alber Elbaz, Alexander Wang, Riccardo Tisci, and Rick Owens, to name a few, to the forefront. She was now a consultant and was focused on sustainable brands. José seemed bored by his seat assignment next to me and started table hopping. That allowed me to move closer to Julie. We spent the night talking and agreed to meet up in New York City the next week. She knew The RealReal and was using the site. I knew she could help us meet the executive teams of the top brands. It was time for me to introduce myself and The RealReal to the executives at LVMH, Kering, and especially Stella McCartney, Alaïa, and Lanvin. And maybe even Chanel, despite its repeated not-so-stealthy efforts to stop The RealReal.

Julie Gilhart and I met in New York City, and I hired her to be a consultant for The RealReal.

The second big recognition: I made the *Vanity Fair* 100, a list of the top one hundred people of the New Establishment. I was number 100, but I made the list. This came as a great surprise and certainly reflected well on The RealReal. I was speaking at the *Vanity Fair* conference in San Francisco in October 2015 and was the recipient of the goodness that came when Graydon Carter was running *Vanity Fair*. That goodness involved being photographed by Annie Leibovitz (a dream come true), a cartoon characterization of me that was placed front and center in a huge twenty-by-sixty-foot outdoor mural that provided an entryway into the conference, and a fortuitous dinner mate at that night's dinner. Other speakers beautifully characterized on the mural included Elon Musk, Lena Dunham, Mark Zuckerberg, and Elizabeth Holmes. Elizabeth Holmes was caricatured in her black turtleneck and was just about to be outed by the *Washington Post*. She was a keynote speaker.

As for the postconference gala dinner, I had asked the women at the door to please seat me by someone interesting and not at the "kid's" table. I am often at the kid's section at these events. They promised me I would be happy. And, as I passed the center tables, the ones with the view of the Bay, I observed Katie Couric chatting with Lena Dunham and Elizabeth Holmes. They were at the cool tables with the important people. I headed to the dogleg section of the Slanted Door restaurant thinking, *Well at least the food is good here.*

As expected, I was seated with the tech people. I knew most of the people at the table, and the person sitting on my right wasn't a small talker. He preferred not to socialize at all. He was known to be super smart and successful and odd. When I sat down, he turned his head toward me, nodded, and looked the other way. Kara Swisher was a few seats down, too far to have a conversation with. The seat to the left of me was empty, and that was the end of the table. I settled into a glass of wine and then, like a burst of tall energy with a golden aura, a person sat down next to me, and I couldn't believe my luck.

Marco Bizzarri, the new CEO of Gucci, was seated next to me. He had taken this position in January 2015, and now in October, Gucci was clearly back on the ascendent. It was on fire. I monopolized him the entire night and pelted him with questions about how he turned Gucci around. I got him to download The RealReal app. I was falling in love. The man sitting across from me knocked on the table a few times and said with a smile, "Hello, I am a very important person, too."

"Really, what do you do?"

"I'm the head of UTA, one of the best talent agencies in the business, and this is my wife next to me."

"You are very important," I said, grinning back at him, "but the man sitting next to me is a god, and I'm a little in love with him right now, so sorry. I'm going back to monopolizing him."

That dinner was epic for me, and it set the stage for future discussions.

In the fall of 2015, I approached Vestiaire Collective, the European self-posting site, to see if there was an opportunity to merge our businesses. Companies that are private and founder run pose challenges for valuation because venture capital valuations are not necessarily tied to the value someone would purchase the company for, and determining senior leadership teams of a blended company is fraught with politics, distress, ego, and drama. But if the will is there, it makes good business sense. There is a solid method for evaluating the company's value based on other comparables—meaning past deals that were done by companies in the same sector or similar sectors. With growth companies, this is a better methodology than profit or earnings per share because there are no earnings, just growth and predictions for profitability. But, quite often, the egos, not the numbers, tend to get in the way of the deal.

In this case, we both signed nondisclosures and started discussions. We shared top-line revenue numbers. The RealReal's revenue was about 50 percent greater than Vestiaire Collective's revenue at the time. The founders at Vestiaire insisted it should be a marriage of equals. The revenue difference shouldn't matter given the growth and impending profitability of their business. However, The RealReal's growth was significantly greater than that of Vestiaire Collective. That discussion went nowhere with them. Their logic was their logic. The numbers didn't matter to them, and they would not move off their position. No deal was done. But we would meet again when they attempted another relaunch into the US market. This time a different type of lawyer would get involved.

It was a longshot to think that we could do a deal, so it not getting done was only a small disappointment. The real disappointment was wasting time with them. When you are growing a company, all you have is time.

We ended 2015 with some great recognition that offset some of the losses. The RealReal and I received awards. Awards are great for a company and a nice surprise when they happen to you, but do not believe your own press. If you believe the good press, you must believe the bad press. Leverage the award for your company and your team and celebrate them. But, as a leader, understand the ephemeral nature of awards. For example, I am convinced that some of the awards I won were because there was a spotlight on the lack of women winning awards. And, so, I was a recipient of an award because someone or some committee needed to fill a quota or right a past wrong. Still, I was happy to receive the award, and because I am human, I was irked when I was overlooked for an award.

And, along those lines, I was the recipient of one of the most prestigious awards in Silicon Valley in February 2020: Silicon Valley Forum's Visionary Award. In my industry, this is considered one of the most important recognitions. Past winners include Bill Gates, Elon Musk, and Reed Hastings. Very few women have won this award, but the 2020 awardees were women and men of color. We represented a very inclusive bunch. I was honored to accept it.

However, my award would be presented to me by Reid Hoffman, a past award recipient and the founder of LinkedIn. He had recently been linked to Jeffrey Epstein. In fact, he had been actively introducing Epstein to many top people in Silicon Valley after Epstein's pedophile conviction. I viewed him as becoming Epstein's advocate. Therefore, I did not want to accept the award from Hoffman and made my rationale clear to the Silicon Valley Forum. This caused the forum a bit of consternation, but ultimately, they let me pick the person to present the award to me. Reid Hoffman was not invited to attend the ceremonies. Did it hurt Hoffman? Absolutely not. He is rich. He is fine. He maintains all his corporate board seats, and whatever his Epstein involvement was, it appears to have had little to no consequences for him at all. Did it hurt me? It could have if I had needed to raise capital from his firm, Greylock, or his friends' firms. Did I feel like I did the right thing? Yes. But there are always consequences for those who take actions against wealthy and powerful people unless you are one of them. I am not one of those people. They have a different set of rules.

Chapter 7

An Epic Fail

Sometime in late 2013, early 2014, a board member, Mathias Schilling, came to me with an interesting idea for expansion. A team of entrepreneurs that had launched Groupon in Japan would be out of work soon because Groupon US had bought Groupon Japan. This team worked in a quasi-franchise mode to launch the Japanese version of the company. Mathias was convinced this team could do the same for The RealReal. I had already explored international as a growth option and had concluded that it was not feasible for us to do it on our own at that stage of the company, but if we did do it, Japan had one of the largest luxury resale markets outside of the United States. The Japanese resale market did not have strong online competition. The vast majority of the luxury resales took place in brick-and-mortar stores around Tokyo.

The board and I agreed to explore this option. The first step was to have the ex-Groupon team visit The RealReal in San Francisco. Mathias organized their trip. Six Japanese businessmen arrived a month later. All were under forty and dressed in chic black suits. I organized meetings with my team, a tour of our operations facility, and meetings with our finance department. They were clearly smart but were not e-commerce experts and certainly had no expertise in fashion. Expertise in e-commerce and fashion could be hired and also gleaned from The RealReal. I decided to explore what a contract would look like. Mathias was my partner in this endeavor.

We reached an agreement with The RealReal funding The RealReal Japan with a $2 million seed investment. This capital would be used to launch the website and hire a team with a focus on hiring a merchant and one salesperson. The overarching goal was to launch the site and then secure investment from Asian venture capital groups.

The RealReal Japan launched a few months later than anticipated. The gating item to launch was supply, and they did not anticipate the resistance to gathering supply. They faced the same challenges I did when launching The RealReal in 2011. It was a new paradigm for con-signing, and new is always hard, especially in cultures that have more fixed ways of thinking about business. Consequently, everything was taking more time than the Japan team anticipated. More time meant more cash was being burned without results.

The RealReal Japan team felt they needed a strong managing direc-tor from the luxury space to help them gain respectability and credi-bility. They had identified an ex-LVMH executive who they wanted to hire. My team met with him and were unimpressed. He did not have an entrepreneurial bone in his body. But it was not our place to over-ride the Japan team's decisions. Our role was to give them feedback. We did, and they hired this person anyway.

Eleven months later, they needed more cash. Sadly, they had achieved minimal traction in the business. A meeting was called where the new Japanese managing director could present his business plan along with incremental funding requirements to the The Real-Real board. The results of this meeting would determine whether The RealReal Japan would get investment from The RealReal's investors. It would be viewed as a separate investment from The RealReal.

The managing director presented a business case that did not address the slow adoption rates of the business and the tactics he would employ to override these issues upon funding. In fact, none of the challenges of the first fifteen months were called out. The RealReal board started asking questions, a lot of questions. None were answered directly. The board members kept at it. The managing director finally blurted out that he did not believe in the online business for luxury resale and stated that he could not compete with the brick-and-mortar stores. And that ended our foray into Japan.

The next week I met with the Japanese team virtually and stated that they would have to begin an orderly shutdown of The RealReal Japan. The RealReal US had to provide incremental financing to support the shutdown. It was a bold experiment that ended in failure. It could have gone the other way, but it would have required great dedication from the Japanese team for problem-solving, passion for success, long working hours, and better talent. Embedding a top employee from The RealReal would have helped, but we did not have the talent to spare. Ultimately, it was probably the wrong time for an expansion overseas, and yet, the execution was worse than the timing.

Chapter 8

Big, Bold Names Meet
The RealReal

The RealReal's newfound fame opened doors that my senior staff and I found a bit surprising. We had no idea people and businesses were paying attention to us. We were just heads down, trying to keep the wheels on the car while we were on the track racing. For starters, every fashion story needs a good Anna Wintour tale. For perspective, Anna is the editor in chief of *Vogue* magazine and a true icon in the fashion industry. In the movie *The Devil Wears Prada*, Meryl Streep plays an editor at a top fashion magazine, and her character is supposedly based on Anna. Simply stated, Anna is a big deal in fashion and is known to have strong opinions about many things outside of fashion, including people. In February 2016, Rati and I happened upon our own Anna experience. We decided to go to London Fashion Week and attend a fundraiser for Hillary Clinton at the South Kensington home of Natalie Massenet, the founder of Net-a-Porter. The event attracted some of the major players in fashion and gave us a great opportunity to network. Because Anna Wintour was cohosting with Natalie, the two women stood at the head of the receiving line, positioned to greet entering guests.

When I introduced myself to Natalie, she was thrilled to meet me. She mentioned more than once how much she wanted The RealReal in London and all the clothing and handbags she had to sell. I almost volunteered to go upstairs and start sorting through her closets then and there. Next up was Anna. I was standing maybe two feet from her, facing her with my hand cordially extended to shake hers. She said quite audibly to Natalie, "Who is this?" Natalie replied, "The founder of The RealReal."

Anna, still looking at Natalie, said, "Ah, right." She never looked me in the eye, weakly shook my hand, and enthusiastically greeted the woman behind me, Anastasia Soare, the founder of the eyebrow emporium Anastasia Beverly Hills. Then Anna posed with her for pictures. Since Anastasia was right behind me, I asked her, "What just happened?" Anastasia smiled and said, "I have over one million followers on Instagram. That's what happened." Even if that was true, it is not that simple to decode Anna, who has been known to cut off people with far more power, money, and influence than Anastasia.

Next, we were shepherded into Natalie's living room and encountered some people we knew. Waiters passed American-style appetizers—mini burgers, spoonfuls of macaroni and cheese, mini hot dogs. We declined all of them, as the invitation indicated there would be dinner, followed by a speech from Chelsea Clinton. Soon we were summoned downstairs for the ceremonies to begin. Anna stationed herself a few feet from the crowd and said, "I hope you all enjoyed dinner." I looked at Rati. She and I were both kind of dumbfounded. Julie Gilhart, the former fashion director of Barneys and now an industry consultant, leaned in and whispered with a grin, "I guess we'll be going out for dinner." And that was the first and last time I met Anna Wintour.

Her bodyguards did get nasty with me, though. I was sitting on Natalie's steps while we waited for the black cab that would whisk us away to a restaurant. One guard said in a very emphatic tone, "Miss Wintour will be coming down these steps soon, and you cannot be sitting here." I told him, "And, when she comes, I will move." They got more aggressive and came toward me. I moved.

Dinner was amazing. About ten of us landed at China Tang, the iconic Chinese restaurant at the Dorchester Hotel. I sat next to Anastasia and heard the story of how she created her billion-dollar business focused on eyebrows. Alber Elbaz, who had just left his post as Lanvin's creative director, and his husband, Alex, joined us, too. It seemed everyone at the table except Rati and I knew how Anna hosted dinner parties.

In September 2016, a call came in for The RealReal's head of communications from Fashion Group International (FGI). The message was simple: Would The RealReal consider being honored as an important rising star at FGI's annual Night of Stars? FGI is a worldwide membership organization serving the fashion, beauty, lifestyle, and retail sectors. Founded in New York City in 1928, FGI is active, respected, and visible within the industry. Others asked to be honored on the same night were Riccardo Tisci, creative director of Givenchy, and Tommy Hilfiger with his wife, Dee Ocleppo. Would we? Of course, we would and wow! It would cost us $25,000 to buy a table. It felt so good, we said we'll take two, thank you very much. We happily invited all our investors, who happened to be primarily female, key employees, and Julie Gilhart, our consultant, to celebrate with us.

I chose a funky black JW Anderson dress for the event. It was sleeveless and tight fitting with a high neckline and an uneven hemline that stopped just above my ankles. Nina García, then the editor in chief of *Elle*, asked to join our table and be seated next to me. I asked my friend Amy Fine Collins to introduce me onstage when I accepted the award. AFC, as she is known, is a writer and former special correspondent to *Vanity Fair*. For more than twenty-five years, during the magazine's heyday, she wrote features about fashion, culture, and society. She also runs the venerable International Best Dressed List, and many designers have regarded her as their muse. When Alan Patricof of Greycroft was considering investing in The RealReal, he asked for her advice on the deal. Even though Alan hated the investment in The RealReal, he still did his due diligence. In doing that due diligence, he approached a fashion industry icon, Amy Fine Collins. Alan then introduced us and said I needed to know her if I was going to succeed in this business. We had become great friends, and she readily agreed to introduce me.

It was a fun star-studded night. One that had an afterglow. As promised, Tommy Hilfiger and Dee Ocleppo accepted a humanitarian award. Riccardo Tisci was introduced by Nicki Minaj. Tory Burch and Pat Cleveland, the amazing model who ruled the runways in the 1970s and beyond and shattered norms because she was Black, were also honored. The next morning the *New York Times* ran a picture of me and my tablemates, Maha Ibrahim, Karolína Kurková, Sonja Perkins, and Magdalena Yesil. Cofounders of a small but powerful Bay Area fund called Broadway Angels, Sonja and Magdalena had made an investment in The RealReal during the fourth round, while Maha's firm, Canaan Partners, had been an early stage investor. And Karolína Kurková was, of course, stunning. Here's a life tip: If you are over fifty and not one of the world's top fashion models, you probably shouldn't stand next to one for a photo op, especially if she is nine inches taller and weighs the same as you.

This is a good time to discuss the luxury industry. There are two main public companies: LVMH and Kering. LVMH, an $86 billion company in 2023, has the following brands in its portfolio: Christian Dior, Celine, Pucci, Fendi, Givenchy, Loewe, Louis Vuitton, Loro Piana, Stella McCartney, Rimowa, Tiffany, Bulgari, Kenzo, Marc Jacobs, TAG Heuer, Sephora, DFS, Belvedere Vodka, Dom Pérignon, and Veuve Clicquot, among others. The second largest public luxury brand, Kering, rang up $21.9 billion in annual sales in 2023. Their brands include Gucci, Alexander McQueen, Saint Laurent, Bottega Veneta, Brioni, Boucheron, and Pomellato. Chanel, a monobrand, was estimated at $17 billion in 2023. Then there is Hermès, also a public company and a monobrand, with 2023 revenue at $14.5 billion. Hermès is mostly a handbag company.

These are large international companies with deep heritages. LVMH and Kering have aggressively acquired brands to balance their portfolio of brands. These are all large, profitable businesses with serious business clout because of the number of employees, advertising spend, and real estate leases/ownership. The industry is in a state of consolidation, with many brands in danger of losing their independence and heritage in order to survive.

This last point was brought home to me when I was asked to speak at a luxury conference in Italy. There was a dinner before the conference where all Italian stand-alone brands like Missoni were present. Bulgari, an Italian brand with a great heritage, had recently been sold to LVMH and were absent from the dinner. So was Gucci. There was heated discussion over dinner about whether stand-alone brands can compete with the conglomerates.

I needed to focus on winning over the conglomerates. The stand-alone brands were all struggling. They could not even spend time or energy thinking about resale.

Julie Gilhart, who had been consulting for us for a while by then, was actively setting up meetings in Paris with LVMH and Kering. She also arranged a meeting with the president of Stella McCartney in London. Our vice president of business development, Allison Sommer, and I traveled to Europe in early November for these appointments. We had been asked to present our business to all LVMH's brand presidents at their normal weekly meeting. LVMH's central offices are located on Avenue Montaigne in Paris, right next to the historical building where Christian Dior founded his couture house in 1947. In the lobby, LVMH proudly showed off its deep heritage with stunning photographs of celebrities wearing Louis Vuitton brands, including Steve McQueen with his TAG Heuer watch and an abundance of vintage Louis Vuitton luggage beautifully displayed behind museum glass.

Our meeting with Ian Rogers—former website wunderkind of the Beastie Boys, ex-CEO of streaming service Beats Music, and now LVMH's chief digital officer—went well. So well that Ian, who looks kind of like Steve McQueen and is from Granger, Indiana, asked me if I had more time because Mr. Arnault, CEO of LVMH, would like a few minutes with me. I was escorted to the top floor into a very large conference room, where Mr. Arnault was seated with Toni Belloni, a managing director of LVMH. Being introduced to a person with the name Toni Belloni, I could not help but laugh a little, on the inside, of course.

Toni was very charming and welcoming and Mr. Arnault, no first name here, was gracious and extremely composed. I remember his posture. Perfect. It made me sit up a bit taller. He explained that he only had a few minutes but that he wanted to meet me. He clearly loved stories of entrepreneurs, as we talked for nearly thirty minutes. I left with the clear impression that he would never do business with us on any level, but he was respectful.

The message delivered indirectly was clear. LVMH leadership explicitly said, but didn't say, that they didn't need us. Some of the LVMH brands had been in existence for more than a century, and they knew they would still be around in another hundred years. Would The RealReal be there in a hundred years? Who knows? That didn't mean I wouldn't try a couple more times.

The next day Allison and I had a meeting with François-Henri Pinault at the Kering headquarters on the Rue de Sèvres. Mr. Pinault's conglomerate, the Kering Group, is housed in a hospital from the 1600s, impeccably restored along with its ancient medicinal gardens. When I walked in the door, I had the same reaction my five-year-old niece had when I took her to Versailles. She wrote in her diary that night, "I could live here." Once you walked through the cobblestone court-yard into the renovated complex, it was a total sensory experience. The inside was modern, done in subdued hues of soft yellow and pale beige, complemented by calm taupes and grays. The catacombs were turned into conference rooms! They were accessed by a spiral staircase and there was a tree growing up from under the ground floor to the reception area. There, a model of the building was proudly exhibited. So were extraordinary sculptures and paintings, each perfectly placed. One would expect nothing less from the man whose holding company owns Christie's.

Allison speaks fluent French, a great tactical advantage for those inevitable impromptu side conversations. On a practical level, her command of the French language got us to our meetings on time as she conversed directly with the taxi drivers. On a subversive level, it offered the opportunity for understanding nuances in conversations happening elsewhere. Although no big secrets were revealed in French while we were present, it gave me peace of mind that we would be ready if they were.

Mr. Pinault's assistant conducted us through the building and up some very small winding steps to Mr. Pinault's office. Dressed in a blue cashmere sweater, slacks, and Gucci loafers, Mr. Pinault was sitting on a couch with two employees to his left. His assistant offered Allison and me the seats across the coffee table from them. The contrast between Mr. Pinault's demeanor and Mr. Arnault's was startling. Mr. Pinault was as relaxed and engaging as Mr. Arnault was correct and formal. Laid out on the coffee table were two binders, one labeled Vestiaire Collective, the name of a French resale business supposedly coming to the United States soon. The other binder said The RealReal.

I started on my pitch. The RealReal is a data-driven company. Because the business is a marketplace, we can predict the trajectory of key brands and key items based on their trending price points over time. With over ten million active members, we can also correlate basket affinities for both the consignor and the buyer. A basket affinity analysis lets you know the brands most likely to be purchased together. That is important for store placement, marketing messages, and competitive positioning.

We had enough data to predict the popularity of a brand, a brand's item type, and what that consumer typically bought within that brand. In other words, we were the canary in the coal mine. We'd know if a brand was on the decline before the brand knew because of the ever-decreasing sales price and the buildup of inventory resulting from increased consignments. We could cut the data by region and by demographic. Of course, we knew the inverse, too. What was hot and what was not were also part of the data we had that brands did not.

We talked about the two other US companies that were changing fashion buying behavior, Stitch Fix and Rent the Runway. Mr. Pinault's charisma was in full force during the conversation, and I became smitten. I could tell Allison was, too. He stated that he thought it was interesting that three women in the United States were potentially reshaping the fashion industry—me being one of them. We talked for more than an hour. My ask of him was to engage in a partnership like the ones we had started with Neiman Marcus and Saks. He said he would support his leadership team if they wanted to work with us, that he had a decentralized approach to management, and that he would encourage his brand presidents to meet with us. As we left, I asked him if I could take the binders on his table to correct any mistakes in his assumptions about The RealReal and Vestiaire Collective. He said no. Then I asked if I could have the small Damien Hirst sculpture on his coffee table. Again, the answer was no. Geesh.

In the taxi heading back to the hotel, Allison, who was maybe thirty at the time, looked at me and said, "He is so good looking in an unexpected way. Those blue eyes! I now see what Salma Hayek sees in him. What a meeting." For perspective, he was nearly thirty years older than Allison. I agreed. I said that I wish someone, meaning Julie Gilhart, would have prepared us for the disconnect between his photos and him in person. Simply stated, his photos do not serve him. His blue eyes were piercing, and he had tremendous charisma, curiosity, and charm. As it related to the business, we left the meeting clearly understanding that we needed to meet with the presidents of the brands as next steps.

Our next appointment, in London, would set the stage for The RealReal to launch worldwide. Allison and I met with the president of Stella McCartney, at that time under the Kering umbrella. The meeting was monumental and the beginning of discussions that went on for six months. Those conversations led to a partnership between The Real-Real and Stella McCartney corporation, which was still ongoing when I exited the company in June 2022.

Stella McCartney's brand is values and conscience driven. She and her team understand the importance of taking care of the planet, and they create a profit-and-loss statement based on how they impact the earth with fashion. Her company has single-handedly driven innovation in renewable fabrics. Her team understands the considerable negative environmental impact the fashion world has from overproduction, a glut that results in landfills of garments with fabrics that may take sixty to seventy-five years to decompose. As they are breaking down, these textiles leach harmful chemicals into the earth. Then there is the sweatshop labor needed to produce fast fashion fabric with a high plastic content that winds up in our water supply and harms animals. Stella McCartney does not use animal products—no leather, no fur, no feathers. She has said that she credits her parents, Linda and Paul McCartney, for her passion for animal rights. This is a luxury brand that does not waver from its focus or bend its values.

Stella McCartney had to approve the partnership. She believes in recirculating goods, she wears previously owned items, and she shops in consignment stores. The business relationship was simple. Stella McCartney would promote The RealReal in her stores through her sales team and collateral material, and when we consigned Stella McCartney items, we would offer the consignor a $50 Stella McCartney coupon to continue to shop at her stores. Our mutual goals were to encourage people to participate in the circular economy. We developed an ad campaign together and their agency came up with the tagline "Make Well. Shop Well. ReSell."

Stella McCartney and her brand are the exception in the fashion industry. EU laws are forcing other European brands to change their practices, but this requires supply chain reengineering, a difficult process.

Given that around two-thirds of our clothes are made from synthetic fibers such as nylon, polyester, and acrylic, the process of simply creating the fabrics releases significant greenhouse gases into the environment, and clothes in landfills accounts for up to 35 percent of primary and secondary microplastic pollution accumulated in oceans, as cited on State of Matter Apparel's website, with supporting data from the European Environment Agency's report by the EEA's European Topic Centre on Circular Economy and Resource Use.

The role of fashion on the planet needs a deeper dive beyond the impact of landfills and production. Fast fashion does more damage than just its considerable impact on the planet. Brands outside of Europe are not regulated. Working conditions and wages are so horrific, they are unimaginable and would be against the law in the United States, Europe, and the UK. And because the workers are often in Asia, the employee conditions are invisible. In 2012, it took a horrendous fire in Bangladesh that killed 112 people who were making cheap garments for sale at Walmart to expose some of these shocking labor conditions. This event resulted in some change in the public awareness and company practices. However, the demand for inexpensive garments has only increased, and there is little to no spotlight on the labor conditions to produce these garments today.

The economics of fast fashion gives you a perspective on the worker's wages. What does the economic model look like to produce a garment that sells for $15, the average selling price on Shein, the fastest growing fast fashion brand in the world? First, there is fabric, buttons, and zippers that must be purchased. Let's say that costs $4 per garment, which is insanely low, by the way, because all of those items had to be made by another factory and shipped to the new location.

Then there is the overhead of the facility and machinery and the costs associated with running that factory—let's say that is $1 per garment. That excludes hourly wages. Then there is management and selling and marketing costs—conservatively, that would be $4 per garment.

If that garment is distributed over the internet, there are internet hosting costs, software costs for security, and other software license fees, which add $0.50 per item. Then there are credit card fees—at this low cost, those would be $0.50. Then there are returns to take into consideration. Internet clothing returns are between 30 and 40 percent, and those returns would have to be handled by a human—let's add $1 to the cost for returns. Then there is shipping that may or may not be subsidized by the vendor. And subsidized shipping costs the vendor another $1. So, now we are left with $3 per item, and we haven't factored in the cost of labor or profit.

There is little to no automation in clothing production. There are still people sitting at sewing machines stitching garments. Assuming one person produces one garment every six minutes, they are producing ten garments per hour without taking a break. Now, let's assume that they are working eight full hours a day outside of breaks, such as for food. That means one could produce eighty garments a day with the average producing slightly less because of machines breaking down and other problems. So, their wage is approximately $0.02 to $0.03 per garment, or maybe $2 to $3 a day, which is $60 to $90 a month. For perspective, the average wage for a garment worker in Bangladesh in 2023 was upped to $113 a month according to the Fair Labor Association, so my calculations are not far off. The rest falls to the bottom line. The average annual salary of a garment worker is less than $1,200 a year. The average annual salary in China in 2023 was over $50,000, but in the manufacturing segment it was $13,700 according to average salary survey and statista.com.

So, what can be done about this? As a consumer, it would be great if we all could be conscious of our choices. But that is not really a realistic request. People need clothes. People like deals. Regulating fashion, especially fast fashion, should fall to the state and federal government. The RealReal started a lobbying effort in 2021 to raise awareness of the environmental impact of fashion, fast fashion in particular. The process is slow. Significant tariffs on cheap imported fast fashion would help. Shareholders holding companies accountable to employee conditions and environmental impact will also help.

And, yes, I did meet Stella McCartney, twice. She is gracious but elusive. How could she not be? But the company she created is not elusive. It is a testament to what can be done when sound ethics drive a company.

The partnership required planning, technical integration, and a coordinated rollout. We agreed to shoot for an announcement on National Consignment Day at the beginning of October 2017.

The idea of a National Consignment Day originated with the marketing team at The RealReal. The concept was simply to declare a day to promote consignment worldwide. We would advertise this event to our customers, issue a press release, convince influencers and politicians to support it, and generally make it a big thing. Ideally, environmentally conscious state governments would make all resale purchases tax-free on National Consignment Day. Though this didn't happen, we did get proclamations recognizing National Consignment Day in New Jersey and New York, and Maryland went so far as to introduce a secondhand apparel tax-exemption bill.

To get a national day, you must buy the rights from a small company in North Dakota. No kidding. One small company owns the rights to a you-name-it national day. So, once we conceived of this special day, we contacted the company and bought the rights because National Consignment Day was still available. Go figure.

Take a moment to reflect on the ingenuity of this business. This company decided they had the right to decree national nonholidays in the United States. And those that bought a day agreed with them. It is kind of magical and crazy. We bought the day because we felt like it should be official. We needed proof of the day even though we made it up. And the firm we bought the day from made it up, too. We did get category exclusivity. No one else can own National Consignment Day.

Rati and I began discussing opening a brick-and-mortar store in late summer of 2016, starting with a pop-up to test the results. We had discussed opening a store from about year three onward so that people could understand the quality and the beauty of the products we were reselling. There wasn't a comparable retail or consignment store in the world that could match what we now had in our operations center. The beauty of running a data-driven, online company is that we would be able to measure the results of a physical store's impact on the business in a given city. Specifically, we could understand if the average order size went up, if the customers who engaged with a brick-and-mortar store changed their buying behavior, if new customers who had shopped at the retail store were as engaged as people who only shopped online, and if there was a general halo effect, a financial lift, in that city resulting from the store's presence. With this pop-up store data, we could then model the business to understand the overall financial impact of adding a true brick-and-mortar store.

I met with my executive team in September 2016, and we decided to do the pop-up in New York City's SoHo neighborhood in time for the holidays. Note the timeline—we decided to do a test pop-up store in September, and we launched it in SoHo in November. Do you know what this is called? It is called getting shit done! And start-ups that can do that smartly and quickly can win.

The sign on the Greene Street pop-up in SoHo read "Shop Until You Drop at The RealReal Pop-Up." And it was an amazingly successful experiment. People who had shopped at The RealReal online flocked to the store quickly. We had emailed invitations to our installed base, so many of the early customers had shopped or consigned with us before. They knew the brand and were excited to shop in our store. Their average order size went up considerably. They brought their friends who had never shopped at The RealReal. Word of mouth kept the store buzzing the entire period it was open. We were so busy, we had a hard time ushering out the customers after our official closing time. We needed to study the six-month impact of the store to understand the true financial payoff, but it looked very promising. Here is what we didn't know and didn't expect: People also came to the store to drop off consignment. A lot of consignment. Now, you may be thinking, *Duh!* Which is what we thought when we did a postmortem.

Of course, people wanted to drop off consignment. That was normal behavior. Yet that was a revelation to us and a new factor to consider when opening a permanent brick-and-mortar store.

We needed to do a two-sided analysis on both consignor and buyer impact. This was a more complicated equation when projecting the financials of opening a store because we had to take into consideration the impact/payment of the sales team for a store drop-off. You may recall that up until this little test, the way we primarily acquired items for consignment was by going to people's homes. I say primarily because we had opened a couple of luxury consignment offices prior to the store test. These were beautifully articulated offices for gemologists, each of whom had the equipment required to give potential consignors estimates on their jewelry and watches.

There were no scribbled messages on a Post-it. There was no leaving the room to talk to a manager. There was one qualified person, The

RealReal gemologist, having a discussion with a potential consignor after a product was evaluated in front of them. A price would then be formally put in writing with a quote that would last six months. This method of consigning brought in nearly half of all fine jewelry and watches. And because we weren't paying for prime retail space, the offices typically turned a profit in less than two months. We also tested that concept before expanding it. The goal was to remove friction from the fine jewelry and watch consignment process and give clients comfort that their items were evaluated fairly. Many people still chose to give their costly possessions to the home-visit luxury manager and some even shipped their valuables directly to our operations center. Opening the luxury consignment offices expanded our supply immediately and was quickly becoming the most important channel for product acquisition for this area of the business. There's that win, win, win again.

Data is critical to all decisions. However, interpreting the data and drawing conclusions are how the data serves the business. I have sat in many meetings where executives do a data dump in a beautiful PowerPoint presentation. Then I ask them: What does that data indicate, what actions should be taken, and how will we measure our success? Even senior executives get stymied by giving their analysis of the data and the indicated actions. There seems to be a fear of making a recommendation based on the data. They would rather just show the data and let a group discussion ensue. According to the consulting firm McKinsey and Company, a large portion of millennials do not like to take risks, as cited in several of their publications on Millennials in 2015 and onwards. Forbes even published an article on May 16, 2019, titled, "Millennials, Fear of Taking Risks Will Hold You Back. Six Ways to Uptick Your Risk Quotient." As a leader, this point is frustrating because if the person presenting the data does not draw the conclusions and recommendations, then this will be done by her or his boss or, worse, the CEO. And the people who cannot draw conclusions, put an action plan in place, and drive results ultimately are not promotable. I spent hours coaching executives on this issue and having them rewrite their presentations to reflect conclusions and indicated actions. This is a skill that is critical for anyone in the business world.

As an entrepreneur, you may not have solid data for a long time. You do have directional data, research, and pattern recommendations, however. For example, when we were deciding where to hire luxury managers for the The RealReal outside of New York, LA, Chicago, and San Francisco, we researched where the luxury boutiques or department stores were located, where the highest-income zip codes were, and what the population size of each key city was. We then made assumptions about the rate of adoption of new trends. The last point was based on my experience introducing new business ideas in the United States. For example, cities in Texas with wealth and population, like Dallas and Houston, are slow adopters. Texans generally like to stick to what they know. Also, movements tend to start at the coasts and move inward. Using these data points and previous experience, we were able to map out hires for the next year and could plan our city-by-city rollout effectively.

Chapter 9

Awards Abuse

I had to raise capital every six months for nine years straight. The CFO did not do any business development deals, though. That was left to me, with Allison as my partner in initiating and closing the deals. I always kept the dialogue going with all luxury brands on two levels.

The first level was doing a simple partnership that would look like the one we did with Stella McCartney. I kept meeting with LVMH and Kering employees in the United States. I met with Anish Melwani, the head of North America for LVMH, who had told me LVMH would never do a deal with The RealReal unless we raised all the Dior handbag prices. Anish is a smart man, and I had reminded him that The RealReal was a marketplace, and the market sets the price, not us. He repeated his demands—or suggestions, depending on your side of the table—and then said, "We will never get a bigger deal done with prices staying like they are."

Of course, we didn't raise the prices. And LVMH was never going to do a deal with us, anyway. Still, the meetings were always instructive, allowing me to keep a pulse on the brands.

The second level was securing investment capital from the investment arm of one of the large luxury conglomerates. Securing capital from a luxury brand would be another sign of integrity for The Real-Real. To that end, a meeting was set up with Mousse Partners, the investment arm of Chanel, in Manhattan. That group works out of Chanel's US headquarters at 9 West 57th Street. The meeting took place in 2016 when our pop-up was active. We were scheduled for a sit-down with Charles Heilbronn, chairman of Mousse and half-brother of Alain and Gérard Wertheimer, the majority owners of Chanel. These two brothers are the grandsons of Pierre Wertheimer, business partner of Coco Chanel herself.

Their offices were on the forty-fourth floor and offered a spectacular panoramic view of Central Park. Large Chuck Close paintings hung in the lobby and, not surprisingly, Warhol's Chanel No. 5 series adorned other walls. Laurent Ohana, who the company had engaged to help us raise strategic money for the next round, had set up the meeting. He accompanied me.

Laurent and I arrived slightly before the 8 a.m. scheduled time and were ushered into a conference room overlooking that bird's-eye vista of Central Park. Charles Heilbronn showed up with an unexpected wingman, their attorney. I had prepared handouts reviewing the background of The RealReal as well as Chanel's indexed numbers broken down by demographic. In other words, I was giving them a look at how their resale prices were holding up compared to a year ago and an analysis of who tended to buy and consign their products by age, gender, and location. Included in this packet was a list of the products those buyers or consignors bought, too. None of the numbers were absolute. They were all indexed versus one year ago or versus similar brands with similar price points. Resale price health is a sign of primary brand health, meaning the higher the resale value, the better the brand is doing in the retail market. When resale values decline, it indicates lack of consumer interest. That interest will be noticeable in the primary market. Therefore, showing indexed values versus one year ago by product type is a valuable piece of information. We used to have pricing analysts do this by hand by top product SKUs. This was later mostly automated by pricing algorithms.

Within minutes of sitting down, Charles popped up, saying he needed to take a call, and left the meeting. Laurent and I remained, facing the attorney. She did not appear to be "on brand," as they say in the fashion industry. She was most likely in her late fifties, and her hair didn't appear to be brushed. She wore no makeup, and her outfit consisted of a baggy cashmere sweater and black pants. The look on her face gave the impression that her features were stuck in a permanent frown, even while talking.

There was an uncomfortable silence after Charles left. Laurent and I looked at the attorney. I glanced at my watch. It felt like five minutes had gone by. She finally broke the silence.

"Let's get started. Would you like some coffee?"

"Yes, I'd love some."

"Get it yourself. It's behind you."

I didn't get my own coffee. I stayed seated.

"Have you visited our pop-up store on Greene Street in SoHo?" I asked.

"Why would I? It's resale," she said, her tone dripping with nastiness.

"I have some data on how the Chanel brand is doing in resale versus other luxury brands. We know that our business is an early indicator of trends given it is a marketplace. Would you like to see the presentation I brought?"

"Your business is my worst nightmare." Her tone had grown more hostile—if that was even possible—and her face had now twisted into a full sneer.

So, this was obviously Charles's plan. What an asshole. He had absolutely no intention of having an investment meeting with Laurent and me. He wanted the attorney to denigrate our business and generally be rude. He wanted to waste our time.

"We're leaving now. I'm not going to stay here and take this abuse." I stood up and left. Laurent trailed behind me. Outside we shook off the bad vibes. I was furious that I had been set up like this.

I view Chanel's people as thugs. They interfered with our ability to have a relationship with Neiman Marcus and Saks, which The RealReal would later address in a lawsuit, and they had blocked our ability to advertise in major publications. And that was just what I knew about. I believed there had been more activity. They seemed threatened by The RealReal. I wondered what they would do next.

A year later, we celebrated National Consignment Day and announced the Stella McCartney partnership. We had taken out a full-page ad in *Women's Wear Daily*, the leading trade paper, to announce the collaboration. We had issued a joint press release with the Stella McCartney corporation. This was big news and received a lot of press coverage. The press team had done a great job of getting the story out. Our employees, now over one thousand, were excited. We celebrated with small parties at all of our facilities.

On the night of October 24, 2017, I walked into another star-studded event, this time at the Pierre Hotel in New York. Rati was with me. We entered the venue at the same time as Marco Bizzarri, the CEO of Gucci, also known as the man I had monopolized at the *Vanity Fair* summit. He looked at me and said, "Your Stella McCartney announcement really shook up the industry." Then he moved on before I had a chance to say, "We could have a similar relationship with Gucci." He left me so quickly that it made me wonder if he was still suffering from PTSD from our first meeting at the *Vanity Fair* dinner. I had thought he was engaged in our conversation since it centered around how he turned around Gucci and rebuilt an iconic brand, but maybe it was only me who loved hearing his story. And, maybe, it wasn't about The RealReal at all. He and Gucci were being honored the same night, and the public relations team was waiting for him to walk the red carpet.

Wearing a short-sleeved, full-skirted Alexander McQueen knit dress embellished with rows of rivets and five-inch-heel Alexander McQueen boots, I took my place on the red carpet as photographers shuttered away. The RealReal was one of five companies or individuals receiving an award at *Women's Wear Daily*'s Second Annual Honors dinner. The other honorees were Karl Lagerfeld, Chanel's creative director, who received the John B. Fairchild Honor; Marco Bizzarri for Creative Leadership; Moncler for the Best Performing Large Cap Company; Patagonia for Corporate Citizenship; and The RealReal for the Best Performing Small Cap Company.

To enter the hotel's ballroom, we first had to walk a red carpet, behind which was a wall covered with dense, velvety clusters of gorgeous red roses. Next came a corridor with a phalanx of eight-foot photos of the awardees. Karl Lagerfeld's picture was first, on the left, and mine was just opposite his on the right. Rati and I were shown to table 1, on the left side of the ballroom, just a few inches from the stage. Karl's table, where he sat with his muse, Lily-Rose Depp, was front and center. At our table were Anna Sui, Vera Wang, three executives from *Women's Wear Daily*, and right next to me, the president of

Chanel, John Galantic. Everyone was already seated except for John, who was paying his respects to Karl.

John joined us eventually. I turned to him and stated that he was going to have an uncomfortable night sitting next to me.

"I wanted to sit next to you," he said.

"I bet you did."

"I hear you had a bad meeting a while ago with some of our people."

"That was a year ago, and yes, your people are some of the rudest people I have ever met. You must be threatened by The RealReal."

"I thought Charles sent you an apology note."

"It was more of a sorry not sorry note."

"Well, then I am here to apologize."

"Okay." I did not believe a word he said. My experience of Chanel was of intimidation. This felt like more of the same to me.

John rose from the table again to chat with some other people. One of the fashion industry executives leaned sympathetically across the table and said, "Don't believe anything he says. Rumor is Chanel tried to get The RealReal's award canceled tonight by threatening to pull all of their *Women's Wear Daily* advertising." Given what I'd already seen—Chanel meddling with our strategic partnerships—it wasn't hard to believe. They were coming at us from every angle.

I accepted the award that night for The RealReal. I never let on that I knew what John had attempted to do. I just carried on with small talk with him.

Anna Sui and Vera Wang were both lovely, and beyond their initial introduction, they did not really talk to either Rati or me. After the awards presentations, Karl appeared onstage in conversation with Bridget Foley, *Women's Wear Daily's* powerful executive editor, for nearly an hour and was really entertaining. Although we shared the same stage, albeit at different times that night, I never went to his table to introduce myself. I didn't know how he would react, and I wasn't in the mood for attitude. Sadly, I would never know. He died about fifteen months later.

Chapter 10

Shaking Up the Fakes

Each year, The RealReal got more and more sophisticated in handling goods to eliminate fakes and root out criminals. That didn't stop people from trying. The RealReal's first warehouse, over 30,000 square feet, was the one on Oakdale Avenue in San Francisco. The space on Oakdale was fitted with cameras spaced out every six feet, and the receiving area was carpeted. These were high-resolution cameras. Lighting was switched out to provide the brightest light possible, except for the photo and photo editing areas. This allowed receivers and authenticators the best possible light to evaluate the items while giving the photo editors a somewhat controlled environment. Later, the gemologists would have a controlled area and special rooms fitted with equipment, but at the Oakdale facility, the gemologists sat with everyone else.

The cameras were critical. Their purpose was to verify what arrived at the operations center and to be able to visually track the movement of product if necessary. Why? Because a small percentage of consignors would say they sent something into the operations center, and it wasn't there when we opened the box. Certainly, it was possible that things were stolen in transit, but pre-COVID that tended not to be the case. Consignors were mistaken. Or they lied. We always assumed they were mistaken, and then we sent them the tapes. There was the possibility of employee theft, too.

Then there were our vendors. From the beginning, The RealReal did business with a handful of vendors to help fill in the gaps of the inventory. We had an ex-banker who became an employee who managed this program for us when we were still in the ICB building in Sausalito. Our vendor policy was clear—we had a zero-tolerance policy for vendors who shipped The RealReal fraudulent products. The first step was to notify the vendor and ask for proof of purchase. This usually resulted in dummied-up invoices. The second step was to notify them that the products shipped to us were fakes, and therefore we would confiscate them. The third step was to terminate the relationship with that vendor and notify the proper authorities.

When this happened, most vendors threatened a lawsuit if we did not return their property. And quite a few of them started down that path. But there were two vendors that really stood out over the eleven-year period I was running The RealReal.

We received a shipment of Prada handbags from a vendor based in California. When the boxes were opened, the smell of glue was overwhelming. The inventory, if it was real, was worth about $350,000 in sales to The RealReal, and it would have netted $245,000 to the vendor. Prada had a very hot handbag that year, and it was in great demand. Further, we needed more high-value inventory heading into holidays. This vendor, the Prada guy, had been working with us on smaller shipments for about four months. Prior to this shipment, his items were authentic. He was clearly chumming us, putting out little bits of real "food" so we would take the bait on the big one. We didn't.

The ex-banker wanted us to send all the product back to him to avoid a lawsuit. But our policy was to confiscate all fake product—so that is what we did. His first letter arrived quickly, demanding the return of the merchandise and threatening legal action.

This was the point in the business when we changed our vendor policy. We had not done background checks on the handful of vendors we had on our roster. We added background checks to our checklist for vendor verification. When we did one on the Prada vendor, it showed that the California company had the same ownership structure as a company based on the East Coast that had been taken to court by Neiman Marcus for providing them with fakes. And the East Coast company lost that lawsuit. Now they had a new name but were clearly in the same business based in California.

After the first letter, another letter arrived from their lawyer, again threatening a lawsuit. Then the daily calls to me and the ex-banker started. Most went to voicemail. The one I picked up was my favorite call. It came from the owner's alleged wife.

"Hello, Julie?" his wife said.

"Yes."

"This is Bonnie. I'm Jim's wife, and I work in the business with him."

"Okay."

"You and I are both technology executives. We have the same background. We have a lot in common."

"Uh, no, we don't. You are a counterfeiter."

"I am sorry you see it that way."

"I see it that way because you sell and maybe produce counterfeit goods. You are a criminal."

"I don't think you understand. We will sue you."

"Okay. We have a lawyer. He will take service. I'll email your husband his name and contact information. He's at Sidley Austin."

They did sue us, but they didn't send the documents to Sidley Austin. It got personal very quickly. Two big thugs pounded on my door one night about a week later. It was close to 10:30 p.m. I know that because my house was under construction at the time, and I was watching *Homeland* downstairs in a spare bedroom. *Homeland* is a very intense show, so I was already stressed out. It was just me and my dogs that night. The goons wouldn't leave. They kept pounding and pounding on the door. There was absolutely no way I was opening that door. I kept looking out the side window to try to see their faces. All I saw were massive, hulky men repeatedly beating on my door. My dogs were going crazy. I called the police, describing the situation with a shaky voice and a cacophony of dog noise in the background. The goons were gone by the time the police arrived. The police handed me the lawsuit, which was pushed partway through my door. I had been served.

It turns out the Prada counterfeiter had a brother who was a lawyer practicing in Florida—a convenient resource when the family's business model is counterfeiting.

The lawsuit was eventually dropped because this guy was a counterfeiter. The RealReal's policy was to turn any counterfeiter over to the FBI or Homeland Security, whoever would take the case. It appeared that our federal law enforcement team had bigger fish to fry because we served them up this guilty little minnow, and nothing seemed to happen. They must have put him at the end of the queue. This company was still posting on Amazon and other sites as late as last year.

Then there was the Canadian con man. We had his fake Valentino scarves. He wanted them back. We said no. He sued. Is it possible every con man has a brother who is a lawyer who will file a lawsuit for them? We were two for two with the lawyer brothers. The Canadian guy turned out to be kind of notorious. Prior to going into the counterfeit business, he was hiring Hasidic Jews to be his drug mules running from New York City to Israel. He was busted in that case but escaped to Canada. He took the lawsuit with The RealReal quite far before he caved. We got to the deposition phase, and we had to send a lawyer to Canada to take his deposition because he had several warrants out for his arrest in the United States. We "settled" out of court on that one, just like every counterfeiter lawsuit that happened under my watch. Unlike any others, his firm paid The RealReal to go away.

Then there were the individual fraudsters. That group is special because its members are always so surprised that we rejected their items because of our inability to authenticate them.

My favorite was the socialite in California who was having her seamstress copy Chanel couture clothing. She is a much-photographed woman. She even sent some of those photos into The RealReal as proof of authentication when the authentication was in question. They were good fakes with some buttons being authentic. If the items were real, we could have sold them for well over $100,000, but they weren't. She wanted her fake Chanel back. We said no. Her husband got involved. We said we were going to notify the police. They went away. We didn't notify the police, but we should have. She tried to consign "Chanel" again about one year later. Her husband wrote a letter to say these were real Chanel items and asked for her to be allowed to sell again with The RealReal. She was blacklisted and not allowed back.

One more story is worth telling here. There was a ring of counterfeiters operating out of Portland, Oregon, that the FBI was interested in arresting. This group was buying authentic items from The RealReal, counterfeiting the items, and returning fakes. It was hard to claw the money back for the returned item after it was refunded.

The RealReal has a general practice that all returned items have to be reauthenticated. However, in many cases, the item would be refunded before it was reauthenticated. We had to tighten our processes considerably. I understand that they fled the country before they were caught.

There were and are fakes entering the product flow daily. While many of our processes had gotten very sophisticated by the time we had over 100,000 square feet of warehouse space in 2015, authentication was still manual. We didn't think we could automate authentication with the fine jewelry and watch pieces, but we knew we could automate authentication for leather goods, including handbags, to some degree. AI and machine learning were our answer. As the company matured, so did our AI and machine learning algorithms. We could detect high-risk consignors and run a first pass on authentication for most handbags by 2022. This is critical when you think of the volume flowing through The RealReal. It was in the high hundreds of thousands per month post-COVID.

No thugs were showing up at my door anymore, either. New thugs would come my way, but they were a different kind of thug and not trying to enter my front door. More on that later.

Adjacent to the fakes were the drugs. This was particularly difficult for The RealReal, and when baggies of mysterious powders were found in the merchandise, it was always a topic of discussion. Truth be told, we didn't know they were drugs. To my knowledge, no one tried them. But they had a high probability of being drugs. We flushed it all down the toilet. In one case, a large quantity of what appeared to be a drug was found in a Louis Vuitton duffel that was consigned. So here is the dilemma: Return the substance to the consignor or dispose of it? We always chose to dispose of it. How would the conversation go if we tried the other path? The call would be something like, "Hello, this is The RealReal customer service. We found what appears to be a ten-pound bag of sugar in the suitcase you consigned. We'd like to send it back to you, but in the event that it isn't sugar, we don't want to go to jail and we don't want you to do so, either. Would you like to pick it up? We are based in New Jersey. No, we can't ship it USPS to Florida." You get the point.

Sex toys were thrown out, too.

Chapter 11

You Can't Stop the Growth

B y the end of 2017, I had raised money six times, five of them with the CFO. The newest investor, Mike Kumin of Great Hill Partners, was the first private equity (PE) investor in The RealReal. Prior to his investment, our investments were from venture capitalists. In 2017, we had Maha Ibrahim from Canaan, Mathias Schilling from e.ventures, Keval Desai from Interwest, Cynthia Ringo from DBL, and Dana Settle from Greycroft as observers. All were investors. Maha, Mathias, and Dana had all invested since 2012. The board meetings were monthly, which is normal in a start-up. The investors got along with each other, and the meetings in general were collaborative. They were helpful to me and my team. The board members really came together when it was time to raise capital for the company, which was every year. Mike Kumin, the latest addition, operated similarly, and he brought a new level of long-term thinking and analytics to our discussions and the management of The RealReal.

Venture capitalists tend to be very good at the earliest stages of business growth. They understand founders, they understand metrics needed to show success, they can help recruit talent, and they can help introduce the founder to other like-minded early-stage investors. Their funds tend to have a long horizon, generally ten years, and the legal terms in term sheets are a common language. I heard someone call this sameness across venture capitalists "exclusionary and discriminatory." That is not true. The documents, and even the law firms retained by start-ups, are built for expediency.

An experienced founder and/or lawyer can quickly look at a term sheet from a Silicon Valley venture capitalist and spot the abnormalities and any extraordinary terms. This allows all to understand the terms that may not be beneficial to the next round of investors and certainly to the founder. What is exclusionary are the venture capitalist firms themselves, comprised mostly of white men with graduate degrees from Harvard, Stanford, or MIT. Most are under the age of forty, with a cluster between twenty-eight and thirty-four. Those are the people making decisions about capital allocation for technology and innovation. And like attracts like.

Not much progress has been made in the structure or processes of the venture capital world except the funds have gotten larger and power has consolidated with a few large players, like Sequoia and Andreessen Horowitz. There have been other changes in investing, especially on either end of the spectrum for start-ups. There are more early-stage investors, and there is a new class of investors attempting venture investing, specifically PE investors. PE investors have a special talent, and that talent does not align with companies in growth mode. I think of them as harvesters and value extractors. They tend to invest in companies whose growth has stalled, then they cut costs to deliver cash back to their investors. They are typically a bad fit with early-stage companies. And, yet, The RealReal had two of them. Consequently, my direct experience with PE investors is limited to two people in two different firms.

One of them was exceptional. Mike Kumin and his firm invested in Series E, our fifth round of financing. Mike was an exception to the rule and did not follow the commonly held views of PE investors. He had deep experience in high-growth start-ups and had an excellent reputation. His approach was different, and his risk profile is different. He was a value creator, not an asset stripper.

When he invested, the business was still in rapid growth mode. We were in a phase where our current physical space was once again limiting our growth. First, we needed to move out of the Oakdale office/warehouse. The smart thing to do would have been to move our operations center to a place that was employer friendly and would welcome a company that created jobs for hourly employees. That was not California's environment, but it was the environment in Arizona and Texas. We should have moved to one of those states, but instead we secured a 250,000-square-foot warehouse space in Brisbane, California. The rationale for staying in California was simple. We had never operated a facility separate from our office, and we were all worried about knowledge transfer and management in a larger facility out of state. We were still evolving our operational processes, and that in and of itself required hands-on management. Plus, all the employees working at the Oakdale facility signed up for a slightly longer commute to get to Brisbane so we could then scale the team with real knowledge workers. It felt like the right decision at the time. But it would have served the business economically on many levels to make the move to another state faster.

We also had to move to a different corporate office. That move was easy. The warehouse had to separate from the NYC office, too. We were running a multimillion-dollar business in an old Midtown office building. We had maybe 18,000 square feet spread across three floors. There were moments when you literally couldn't move until someone else or something else moved first. We secured a 110,000-square-foot warehouse in Secaucus, New Jersey, across the parking lot from the Kering warehouse.

The empty spaces both excited me and scared me. We had done the math and knew the amount of space we needed to support our growth for the next two to three years, assuming an aggressive growth rate of 50 percent per year. That should have comforted me, and it did to some degree. But every time I walked into an empty space, I kept imagining the amount of product we would need to fill it. Then I would back that into how many salespeople we would need, how many receivers, how many authenticators, how many gemologists, shipping people, and so on. The numbers were thrilling and scary.

Also, the pop-up had done so well that we had started looking for a space for the first The RealReal permanent store. That was an interesting process. There was an overabundance of empty NYC retail storefronts even then. But many, in fact most, would not rent to us. The landlords didn't want a "pawnshop" in their neighborhood. Explaining the difference between The RealReal and a pawnshop was oddly hard, especially to this target audience, because first you had to explain shopping on the internet to them. Did I mention that it was 2017?

We found our space at 80 Wooster Street in SoHo. The place had been empty for a long time, and the landlord seemed open to taking a chance on our concept. We were thrilled, as the street was reinvigorated with Gucci leasing a large retail space at the end of street, and Celine was across the street.

The next physical space we had to expand was our office in Los Angeles. We had grown from six salespeople to nearly thirty people.

No one had space to sort their goods for shipment. And we needed to open a luxury consignment office. We found an ideal spot in Century City on Avenue of the Stars.

Rati oversaw all merchandising on the site and all stores. I had marketing, finance, sales, operations, and technology reporting to me. For the store and pop-up executions, she had identified the merchant she had hired to run the fine jewelry and watch category as the right person to roll out all the stores and pop-ups. Some people show their ability to scale quickly. He was one of them. He joined the company from a jewelry store in Boston where he was a salesman. We were still at the Oakdale office, which was cantilevered over the warehouse space. Every day for the first three months, he would show up in a suit. He would often start a conversation with words like "in my experience."

One day I just couldn't take it anymore and said, "In your experience? Aren't you twenty-two years old?" Actually, I probably said, are you *twelve* years old? He said, "No, I'm twenty-six." Okay, then. Despite all his annoying experience, he was the type of employee who would run through a wall if that was the only way to get something done. He mostly knew when to ask for help, was conscious of timelines and budgets, and was a creative problem-solver. His ability to get stuff done combined with Rati's store and merchandising experience resulted in minor miracles and beautiful stores.

For example, we had a not-so-minor issue with the tenants that lived above the Wooster store. That area in SoHo is historic, and in the 1960s many artists squatted in the buildings and then eventually were able to buy their apartments. Alex Katz, a famous artist in his nineties, still works out of his SoHo studio nearby. The RealReal's location, 80 Wooster, was a former art gallery in the 1960s and 1970s that Warhol, John Lennon, and Yoko Ono frequented. Consequently, we had a set of grumpy artists above the store. They had voted to approve the rental to The RealReal, but they didn't like us being there. One of the residents would act like the project supervisor and visit the construction site, take notes, and regularly call the city on us. The head of the store roll-outs found common ground with them and completed the project.

The SoHo store opening night party was a fun celebration of hard work. We hit our dates, even if some of the paint was still wet. Laura Brown, the fashion editor of *InStyle* magazine at the time, showed up, as did Jessica Seinfeld. Did we have to pay them to do so? Not Laura—we had to give her an exclusive on the story. Jessica required a donation to her charity, which helps moms and children in New York City. Not a hard charity to support. Our investors dropped in, and our customers and all local employees were invited. The next day, the store was packed. And, once again, people were wheeling in bags of consignment. This time we were ready. The upper floor was all women's fashion, but the downstairs area was men's fashion, a coffee bar, consignment offices, and an outdoor courtyard. The consignment offices were staffed with gemologists who could also quote on handbags. Luxury managers were meeting their clients there. Within months it became clear that the value of the stores would be measured on both product acquisition and selling high-value items, just as the pop-up store had indicated.

New Yorkers like to stay in their neighborhood. When I asked one prominent Upper East Side woman if she had visited our SoHo store, she asked me if she needed a passport to go downtown. We were not getting any of our customers or really anyone from the Upper East Side down to SoHo. Within a few months, we started looking for another space on the Upper East Side and again encountered the pawnshop issue. But this time we could invite a prospective landlord to visit the SoHo store and have a coffee with us as we discussed our plans. We ended up in the former Celine store on the corner of Seventy-Second and Madison. The store had a much smaller footprint than the SoHo store, but it had a beautiful, dramatic staircase that took you up to the consignment offices. The ground floor allowed for a great display of fine jewelry and handbags with limited space for clothing. There wasn't enough room for a men's department. Within a year, that store was beating SoHo on dollars generated per square foot. Location matters.

Locations for a store in Los Angeles were also being scouted. We decided to rent a larger store on the corner of La Cienega and Melrose, and after a lengthy negotiation, it became a hard hat area by July 2018. This West Hollywood location allowed us to test curbside service drop-offs for consignors in the back, even more consignment offices, a larger men's section with a sneaker dome, a men's watch section, and an expanded handbag and fine jewelry area in the women's section. The goal was to open it before the summer ended. Fall was always a big buying and consigning time.

I flew in to inspect the action at the West Hollywood store as it was under construction, and I knew it was going to be a true showcase given the light, ceiling height, and size. These were exciting times with everyone focused on the same goals. There was a feeling that we were building something special, and we were. We were also on a mission to get people to consign and do good for the planet. Our stores had messages on the walls inviting people to join the circular economy. We knew it sounded ephemeral to discuss the circular economy, so we started researching how we could quantify the real impact of consigning. We were also on a mission to find ways to actively measure the carbon and water impact of recirculating goods versus buying new.

My next stop, the same day as my LA store visit, was Las Vegas. We were holding our Annual Worldwide Sales Summit over the weekend. The first was in 2013 at the Casa Madrona in Sausalito. There were about nine of us, me included. Every salesperson at the first sales summit had been put to work during their interview. In the early days, it was hard to interview people and still get all the orders out and the customer service calls done by day's end. The jobs we were interviewing for were mostly in the sales area, and our candidate pool tended to come from either Neiman Marcus, Saks, or another luxury brand. Retail sales positions are considerably different from the luxury manager positions we needed to fill. The overlap was clear—we did want people who understood luxury product and luxury clientele and knew how to sell a service. The jobs diverged in every other way possible. We were looking for people who were entrepreneurial, who didn't mind doing the physical work of removing goods from people's homes, inspecting the goods, cataloging them, and then shipping them to an operations center. We needed salespeople who were risk-takers, loved to work independently, and especially at the beginning, didn't need a full-time boss, since their boss was me.

When we were interviewing sales candidates in the first three years, either Rati or I would stop the interview and ask the person if they wouldn't mind helping us pick, pack, and ship orders. Then either Rati or I would teach them how to pick an order and where to stage them. One candidate was so tiny in stature that I thought we had lost her in the racks. I remember calling down to her, "Hello, are you still down there?"

"Yes, I'm still picking orders."

"Good, phew."

Then there was our future employee from North Carolina. She wanted to shut her consignment store down and join us. She had gotten in touch with me through the customer service email, which I was still answering when needed, and we flew her out to interview. She brought three bags of consignment. I asked her if she could change her flight back home and help us work all weekend on a large consignment pickup at a San Francisco client's second home in Pacific Heights for her clothes and jewelry. She wanted to sell that house and had decided to consign over a thousand items. Let that sink in.

She agreed and went to work. We made her an offer during her working interview. Our first Chicago salesperson, also a very early employee, got off easily. She only had to work in the warehouse for an hour and then we took her out to lunch at the infamous Seahorse restaurant.

The work exercise was a good test. It turned out to be a good predictor of success in the field. Having someone who is flexible, willing to jump into a situation that they knew nothing about, and get the job done well, all the while enjoying the process, could be evidenced by having these candidates pick, pack, and ship orders instead of discussing the position with us. Unorthodox hiring practices can work for positions that are not formulaic. The key is to map the traits needed, ones that are better demonstrated than discussed, with the tasks at hand.

By 2018, we had come a long way from the top nine employees who had survived the pick, pack, ship exercise in Sausalito. By then, we needed one of the largest ballrooms in Las Vegas to host our National Sales Summit. Over 450 salespeople from all over the United States would be attending. We settled on the largest room at the Bellagio Hotel.

The head of sales wanted to make this year particularly special. Our goal was to exceed $1 billion in top-line revenue, and we had $1 billion within our sites within a year. The whole management team flew in for a day of presentations. Every department head was excited to discuss their plans and involve the sales team in their department's goals, answer questions, and actively participate with the sales team. The summit was structured to reward salespeople who had consistently made their quota throughout the year. There were three days of meetings, two nights of fun, and then back to work, hopefully more energized and excited about the company and their jobs. The head of sales wanted to recognize the top performers in an impactful, exciting way.

Dubbed The RealReal Oscars, the last night was the awards night. Everyone walked the red carpet to enter the ballroom, with photographers flashing away and asking people to look at them for their photo. Once inside, the energy was even more electric. This sales team did not look like a technology sales team. The team was mostly women from the ages of twenty-five to seventy-five dressed to impress, excited to be with their other team members. Most worked out of their homes. These were fashion-loving people, and the men in the group really brought it, too.

After a few drinks and dinner, the head of sales took the stage and announced the first winner. Small gold statues were arranged on the table behind him. The winners really enjoyed themselves. One man from New Jersey thanked three of his consignors for getting him over the hump and having regular monthly pickups. One woman was speechless, saying she had never won any award ever and that she was calling her mom that night. One dedicated her award to her dog because he never complained about the long hours she worked.

To reinforce our near-term goal of hitting $1 billion in top-line revenue, the marketing team had $1 billion bills made with my image on them. There were piles of $1 billion bills on every table. The bills were the same size as a dollar bill and the ink color was similar to a real bill. Everyone grabbed a few $1 billion bills as they exited the venue, me included.

About one month later, I was traveling to Canada and was singled out for a security check that was so comprehensive that it stopped just short of a body cavity search. I had The RealReal's $1 billion bills in my wallet. As we all know, people working in airport security take their jobs very seriously. They have to. And they don't appear to have a sense of humor.

"What is this?" the TSA guard asked me as he pulled two of the bills out of my wallet.

"Oh, right, um, well, I run a company, and we are trying to hit $1 billion in revenue, and this was on the tables at the sales meeting to inspire people."

The TSA guy measured the bills versus other real money in my wallet. "It is illegal to counterfeit currency."

"Sir, please look at this bill. It has a woman's picture on it—mine. When has there ever been a woman's picture on any bill? Let alone a bill that says 'one billion dollars' on it? We weren't trying to counterfeit anything." (Please note the irony there.)

"You have a point about a woman's picture on money. This picture doesn't look like you, though."

"I know, I photograph beyond recognition. Could I have my billion dollars back, please?"

With that, the TSA guy handed me my wallet and my two $1 billion bills, and I was allowed to continue to the gate.

The main goal of this exchange was to keep myself out of some windowless interrogation room for hours, which would have resulted in missing my flight. My tactics worked, but he didn't pick up on the underlying feminist statement, which is probably a good thing. I wasn't trying to be clever. I was trying to point out that it couldn't be a forgery. However, I did try to keep my tone flat when I talked to him because, in my head, I was thinking, *Come on guy, look at the picture. Women still have not made it onto the American symbol of success—our money. We barely got our faces on postage stamps. Do you have a daughter? Do you have a wife? Do you understand that we aren't there yet?*

I swear I had all of that bottled up inside of me when I made that statement, and it was just waiting to burst forth if he hadn't agreed with me. When I boarded the flight that day, I realized that the constant struggle of being a woman in business and being dismissed had gotten to me, and I needed a break or a better way to cope. I couldn't take one, though. Too much was happening. I'd have to find a few more minutes every morning to just be quiet—maybe that would work.

There is a term that has crept into the business lexicon that describes slights against a minority group: *microaggressions*. The business impact on the individuals affected by microaggressions is tough to measure. It also feels like one of those terms that can be co-opted and used or politicized without understanding the meaning of it. A few employees complained to The RealReal's human resource department about daily microaggressions, which always triggered an investigation and some form of remedy. There is a general feeling among many that microaggressions have a micro impact. This is simply not true for anyone experiencing them repeatedly over the years. McKinsey and Company releases an annual report on women in the workplace. The October 2023 report cited that "the workplace is a mental minefield for many women, particularly those with marginalized identities. Women who experience microaggressions are much less likely to feel psychologically safe, which makes it harder to take risks, propose new ideas or raise concerns." The report gives further insight into the situations all women face that are only heightened if you are a woman of color, have disabilities, or are a member of the LGBTQ+ community. The data McKinsey provided supported the comments and feedback we were receiving at The RealReal.

Now you may be asking yourself, why would a female CEO running a company heading toward $1 billion even identify with these issues? Simply stated, because I dealt with them daily, too, and certainly had dealt with micro- and macroaggressions throughout my career. I was and am constantly making attitude readjustments to offset what happens to me personally. Some days it works, and sometimes the cumulative effect of past issues spills over inappropriately to someone like a security guard who is just doing his job.

As we rolled into the fall of 2018, recognition continued, but this time for me. *Entrepreneur* magazine had named me as one of the 50 Most Daring Entrepreneurs of 2018 along with Elon Musk, who was on the cover, and *Inc.* magazine had cited me as one of the Top 100 Female Founders. And, closer to my roots, my alma mater, Purdue University, called and asked me to be honored as an Old Master, which I graciously accepted, but I did ask them to consider dropping the "Old" part. They didn't change the name.

As 2018 progressed, I was extremely conscious that at some point The RealReal would need an exit strategy for our investors. When you take in outside investors, they must get their money out, hopefully with a multiplier on the original amount that went into the company. The earliest investors had invested more than seven years ago. Most early-stage venture capital funds are set on a ten-year clock. The clock was ticking for The RealReal to deliver a financial outcome for my earliest investors and for their limited partners. Another way to provide exits for investors is a merger. There were no obvious buyers for The RealReal. The other resale players were too small and private, and they would not deliver significant economic benefit because the business models were too divergent. The large luxury houses had not embraced a multibrand business like The RealReal and, in general, still had no appetite for a resale business. There was only one solution. The RealReal needed to go public.

I raised the issue of going public in 2019 at the fall 2018 board meeting. The business had become highly predictable. The path to profitability was clear. Everyone agreed with my recommendation to go public. No one agreed with my recommendation that we needed to replace our current CFO with a more experienced person. Specifically, I felt strongly that I needed a CFO with public company experience. No one disagreed with my rationale, but one key member argued that there was not enough time to make this hire and go public. The others supported that person's point of view. I was overridden.

In my strong opinion, this was the wrong decision, and I should have insisted that an experienced CFO be by my side. It ultimately was my mistake. I also understood the board's rationale for not hiring a new CFO. We did not have a lot of time to bring a new person up to speed. The company had gotten more complex with the introduction of additional product lines and retail stores. Further, the dynamics of a resale business—specifically retail dynamics—were different from companies the public market analysts were familiar with. A main role for a CFO is to clearly explain their business to the analyst community. Further, it is important to suggest to the analysts what companies another company is similar to, so the analysts could view any company's financials vis-à-vis similar companies. This should be a fairly easy job for a CFO. Most companies fit nicely in a category.

However, this requires tremendous skills when a company is really in a new category. Think of how hard Amazon was to explain when they went public in May of 1997. There were no precedents for what they were doing. Clearly, The RealReal isn't as earth-shattering as Amazon was at the time, but it is a marketplace unlike others that were already public. Being hard to peg is not an asset in the public markets, and The RealReal was one of those companies and was very hard to map to others. This is all to say that I should have insisted that I had a more experienced team by my side when the company went public.

Diving deeper here, The RealReal business was highly dependent on the quality of the inbound supply, but it is not dependent on one single brand. For example, if Ralph Lauren or Michael Kors has a bad year, analysts can point to the creative director not hitting the market or over distribution of secondary lines. These metrics did not apply to The RealReal. So a comp to a luxury brand or luxury brand group does not work. Then there was Farfetch. It had luxury brands like we did, and it was a marketplace like we were, but it was not a resale business. Still, we knew we would be compared to it since there were some similarities, and in the last part of 2018, its stock and growth was on fire. Like The RealReal, it still was not profitable. I was worried about Farfetch's business model because it had lots of restrictions on pricing and product when working with the brands and could not alter its price/product selection without brand approval. And its spending was out of whack for its size, especially in technology. I felt that if Farfetch were the only true comparable in the market, our stock would slide when they hit a rough patch. That is unless we had an experienced public market CFO telling our story. It is all about the story one tells and the results that support that story.

Although I didn't feel good about the decision to go forward on the initial public offering (IPO) without a new, more experienced person leading the financial team, I did embrace us going public. And, oddly, for the first time in a long time, I felt good about my personal life. I had been dating my neighbor. He was fun, kind, and funny. His eyes twinkled when he discussed architecture and technology. He had a very dry sense of humor. Being with him became a safe place to relax, given all the craziness that was about to happen. We could spend a rainy day reading and not talking until it was time for dinner. We both loved hiking. We both loved being on the water. I am enthralled with architecture, and he was a great building guide when we escaped to Europe, which we managed to do a couple of times.

Chapter 12

The Dream, the Money, the Drama

The process for going public is fairly uniform for all companies. The first step in any pre-IPO process is putting together a representation of the board members to listen to the bankers' pitches and recommend to the board the best bankers to tell a private company's story and take it public. The second step is preparing documents for bankers and inviting the bankers to pitch for the business.

The CFO placed calls to the bankers we had met along the way and invited them to participate in a formal IPO pitch process. The bankers' pitch meetings were very interesting. The bankers' goal is to tell management how they would position the company, how their expertise is different from other bankers, and how that expertise will uniquely benefit the company. Secondarily, they use their pitch time to introduce the banking members who would be working with the company to write the S-1 document and subsequently sell the shares into the public market. The only bank that declined to pitch was J. P. Morgan.

We set aside more than two weeks to hear the pitches. There are two banks that are juggernauts in technology IPOs—Goldman Sachs and Morgan Stanley. J. P. Morgan is a close third. There used to be a commonly held belief in Fortune 500 companies that no one ever gets fired hiring IBM. Goldman Sachs and Morgan Stanley were the IBM of IPOs. We had already worked with Kim Posnett of Goldman Sachs in another capacity, and I personally was looking forward to working with her again on the IPO. The day of the pitch, Kim literally phoned it in and sent in her junior team with her calling in on a speakerphone that had a bad connection. It felt like a clear signal that Goldman was not interested. They were out.

Morgan Stanley, led by Kate Claassen, did an amazing pitch. Kate was also a consignor and understood what The RealReal did. However, some of us could not get past the fact that they also represented Poshmark, a low-end self-posting site reportedly also readying to go public. According to my investors, the Poshmark management team had been known to trash talk The RealReal within the investment community. We passed on Morgan Stanley for that reason.

The surprise win went to Credit Suisse as the lead and Bank of America as the second. Both banks worked hard to win the deal, and their presentations were stellar. Banks can make millions of dollars in fees taking a company public. The banks that win the assignment are also well positioned to get future business for any banking needs, from raising convertible debt to mergers and acquisitions. The committee's recommendation back to the board rattled a couple of board members. One in particular said we were making a mistake by choosing Credit Suisse. But the majority of the board voted to accept the committee's recommendation, and we moved forward.

We hired Lise Buyer of Class V Group to help us negotiate the nuances of working with bankers and the IPO. Lise and I had met when she was a vice president of T. Rowe Price and I was CEO of Berkeley Systems.

One of the critical next steps after the bankers are chosen is for those bankers to hear presentations from every executive at the company. Those presentations provide the background of the executive, a description of the functional area they manage, their direct reports, their goals, and their challenges. For us, it was a long, all-day meeting. We decided to hold our meeting at our operations center in Brisbane so the banking team could get a deep understanding of how we process and authenticate the products. My team was a bit jittery in anticipation. Not because they were worried—they were all still wrapping their heads around what was happening. The RealReal management team couldn't know that we were proceeding toward a public offering until we—the CFO, the bankers, the board, and I—were fairly far down the road. It needed to be confidential. Leaking to the press or a competitor would have hurt the company.

The all-hands meeting with the bankers brought exciting facts into focus: The RealReal was really going public. Most of the original executives were still with the company, with some exceptions. The CTO was now Fredrik Björk, who had been at the company for more than seven years and in the role of CTO for about four years. The previous two CTOs had exited a while before. The head of sales was relatively new to The RealReal, but he was a seasoned sales executive. Other than that, the team had been there for years. This felt like a dream come true for everyone.

We had commandeered a large open space off the operations center for the meeting. The executives were at the front of the room. The banking teams, about fifty people in total, sat in seats facing us. It was showtime, and I was pumped. I loved talking about The RealReal and presenting the business. I was ready to go, but one person on the The RealReal IPO team was late. We started without her.

Lise slid into the back of the room about fifteen minutes into the meeting. I had been talking her up to Rati and the head of marketing. She is a true talent, and I trust her advice. When she walked into the meeting, she had a large black eye patch over one eye. Without missing a beat, the head of marketing whispered to Rati and me, "Oh my god, we are being taken public by a pirate." I started giggling and had to suppress that feeling every time I looked at Lise, which was pretty consistently throughout the day. Let's agree that a giggling CEO is not something bankers were used to, but a pirate in a sea of bankers who mostly dress and look the same *is* funny.

The day concluded with all in the room feeling excited about the deal. After this meeting, the detail work started, in which large groups of bankers and their lawyers, the company's lawyers, and the independent lawyers would start meeting three times a week.

The activities leading up to the IPO are standard and involve lots of lawyers and bankers and meetings and the SEC at some point. The goal is to write a solid, somewhat selling S-1, also called a red herring, that explains what the company does, why this company is unique, what the total market opportunity is, what the competition is like, publish financial data, and most important, what the risks are. This document is then on file and should be read by every prospective investor. The risk section of an S-1 is always substantial and meant to cover every possible issue. It really is a cover-your-ass section. We didn't have a risk of pandemic in our S-1. No one did. I bet it has been in all S-1s hence.

As the date approached for our IPO week, the key analysts from the banking side were brought over the wall. These analysts are exposed to the company's projections in detail and a set of financial assumptions that will drive the business. They saw a financial document that projected the financials for the balance of 2019. Specifically, they got a go-forward profit-and-loss document that is the business's projections by month for the balance of the year with two to three years of historical information included. Once they had this data, they asked a few clarifying questions. Then they wrote an independent assessment of the deal, which we and our bankers did not see. This happens to every company going public. This is a critical step, and if a company performs to the financial projections that were shared, it helps build overall credibility with the analyst market. Unfortunately, the information the analysts were provided from The RealReal financial team had a significant error in the calculations due to simple spreadsheet error that was not caught before the documents were sent. Once that issue was discovered, the old documents had to be recalled and a new set of numbers submitted. This made the bankers nervous, and at least one of my board members was furious. It certainly wasn't the best way to build initial trust with the public market analysts.

Once the SEC had approved the S-1, we began the process of marketing the deal to potential investors. We started on the East Coast with three to six meetings a day. The bankers were in every meeting assessing the investor interests and building their book. We flew in and out of cities for ten days with the hallmark moment of a forced overnight in Baltimore due to a mechanical issue. And we had to "stick to the script" because all people must hear the same thing. I received the most warnings about this. I had to constantly keep myself in check. I love this business, and I knew it better than anyone. The numbers, the trends, the key levers—I knew them cold. I am blessed with a pretty good visual recall for numbers, so I could nail most questions without hesitation. Mathias, our Series A investor, was better than me, but he wasn't on the roadshow. It was the CFO, me, and Credit Suisse or Bank of America bankers. We had an SEC- and lawyer-approved PowerPoint presentation with the highlights from the S-1. Then we would take questions. We had several dress rehearsals before we left for the roadshow. Those dress rehearsals included role playing and question-and-answer sessions with the bankers and lawyers.

Once we had built our investor base, the next step was the IPO. Like everyone going through this process, we had scheduled it a day ahead of time. This felt more nerve-racking than it should have because, at the time, it felt like one tweet from President Trump could result in market volatility, which could then result in The RealReal failing to get a good pop in the market. I had already played out the potential headlines in my head: "The RealReal Doesn't Get Any Real Investors." "The RealReal Didn't Really Convince the Market." My holdover PTSD from the Pets.com headlines—"Pets.com Goes to the Dogs" and "Pets.com Fails to Deliver"—made me nervous about reliving those moments with The RealReal.

The day of the IPO finally came. Originally, there was worry among the banking community that WeWork would attempt an IPO in the early fall, and that could have shut the market window. WeWork had extremely challenging financials and an unpredictable founder. More than one banker said we had to move quickly. There might be an investor backlash against not-yet-profitable companies if they attempted to go to the public markets for financing. And The RealReal was a not-yet-profitable company.

All employees who had been at the company for more than five years and their significant others were invited to attend the IPO. The company had secured a great rate at a Hilton within walking distance of Nasdaq. I was staying at the Andaz across from the New York Public Library and a short walk to our office on Thirty-Sixth Street. I had the taxi drop me a couple of blocks from Times Square at 6:56 a.m.

on June 28, 2019. I took a picture of the clock in Times Square so I could lock the memory into my brain. The man I was dating had traveled with me, but I had to get to Nasdaq early and didn't want to have him come with me and then wait around. Plus, I wanted to walk to Nasdaq by myself and savor the moment. He was meeting me there a couple of hours later. I walked slowly toward the building. The streets smelled of urine. A few tourists were milling about, and homeless people were pressed against the alcoves of the businesses. It was already hot and stinky, like June days in New York City can be. The Nasdaq's large screen was showing an advertisement for New York City. Soon, it would be all about The RealReal.

I walked into the building, through security and past the area where we would be pressing the button. REAL, our stock symbol, was there in the plasma screen header, followed by the words "Initial Public Offering." I signed in, got my badge, and walked past the fraternity wall of pictures of CEOs who had taken their companies public. No women were represented. I would be only the twenty-third female founder to take a company public. A hallmark, maybe, but a sad one, for sure. I was ushered upstairs to a briefing room along with some Nasdaq executives and my press team. The office was on the second floor, and I could see my friends and family along with all employees and their families as they entered through security below. All The RealReal investors were there, including Alan Patricof, who had chastised me all those years ago. Within a year of Greycroft's investment, he had come around and was a big supporter. I was pleased he made it to the event. Somehow, turning him around was more gratifying than it should have been.

There was a breakfast at 8 a.m. where the CEO of Nasdaq, Adena Friedman, would say a few words and then I would. Adena leaned over after her talk and said to me that she had never seen such a stylish, diverse, inclusive, and large group for an IPO. She took note that we had people across the company represented. She said the last company that had gone public had ten men present. She was correct about The RealReal. We were all that. We were also passionate, and if you took me out of the equation, young.

Then at 9:15 a.m. we made our way to the place where I would press the button at 9:30 a.m. The room was electric. The entire management team and their families gathered on either side of me. Rati was to my right, and the rest of the executives were to my left. Then the clock ticked 9:30, I pressed the button, and we were public. Confetti dropped from the ceiling; people cheered. Hundreds of pictures were taken. My favorites are with the management team cheering and the one with all the female investors. We did it. We really did it. It was a heady day. I was so proud of my team, my investors, all the employees. I was thanking so many people, I almost forgot I still had responsibilities that day.

The large Nasdaq screen facing Times Square announced we had gone public. We were simulcast on the screen towering ten floors. Our commercial played on the screen. We took more pictures inside, we took pictures outside, we took pictures everywhere. The stock opened high, giving The RealReal a $2.1 billion market cap.

Every employee had stock in The RealReal. That was a mandate from me and the board. This meant every employee could get a good to excellent bump in their net worth. Everyone also had to abide by the rules of only selling after the six-month lock-up period and only selling within an open window. No employees, including executives, sold during the IPO process. Stock was another reward for working hard. Our jill-of-all-trades and one of our first employees, Maria, bought a condo with her money. Others made a down payment on a house. It was extremely gratifying to be able to provide that for all employees, who were mostly women and many minorities.

I was ushered off for press meetings. At some point, my voice gave out and I could only answer questions via texts. I returned to the hotel around 5 p.m. We had to get ready for the IPO party that night. It was Pride Week in New York City, and we had the perfect band: the Village People and their opening act, Sister Sledge. It was a hot, sweaty night, and we danced it away. Sister Sledge delivered that night. The Village People were fine.

I left around midnight. I was exhausted, and so was my date. Others went clubbing all night long.

I've always had boundless energy—a true gift if you are an entrepreneur. I've never really been sick, and I've never been overly tired. I get up early every morning, and I am ready to go. I am the consummate annoyingly chipper morning person. But not the day after the IPO. I was bone tired, and my voice hadn't come back. I had a meeting with Burberry in London to discuss a partnership two days later. They were ready to discuss how we could do a Burberry deal that worked for both companies. I needed to be ready.

I flew out to London and checked into the Ned Hotel. The Ned is kind of odd and wonderful at the same time. It was once a bank, and the offices were converted into rooms. There are several spots in the hotel where live music is played. My favorite is The Vault, where you go into the vault of the bank where the safety deposit boxes have been polished to reflect the low lights on the tables, and there is usually a jazz or blues band playing. The Ned is affiliated with Soho House, but unlike other Soho House properties, it does not require a membership. The Soho is an interesting venture and was a true start-up. It managed to create unique properties curated for a specific audience in London and then replicate the formula across the world. I've been going to Soho House properties in London for years. It has been fascinating to watch how they have expanded. That business is a testament to having a unique vision that is culturally and socially relevant. I've seen them grow from a dining club to a club with hotels, cinemas, spas, full dining, and products. I tend to stay at Soho properties when I travel to see how the business has innovated and improved its offering. It is a dynamic organization.

Burberry's headquarters was located next to MI5's headquarters in London. That in and of itself was kind of fascinating. I know this because my cell phone was blocked during my visit, and a Burberry security guard explained it to me. The Burberry office was very chic and white. The atmosphere felt good even though the company was coming off a couple of bad missteps. In mid-2018, Burberry reported in its annual report that it had burned £28.6 million ($38 million) worth of overstock goods. The company said it needed to keep the value of the brand up. Activists' groups were in an uproar. Social media activity was extremely, relentlessly negative on Burberry. By early September, Burberry was making promises to stop the burning of overstock goods and stop using real fur. It was in the mood to recast itself as an environmentally sound brand. Burberry management thought The RealReal could be part of the brand's environmental solution. We thought Burberry was a fine company to work with. Our goals were aligned. Consequently, the Burberry meeting went extremely well. We agreed to develop a partnership to encourage the circular economy and planned for a fall release. I left the meeting with concrete next steps and felt great about the impending partnership.

Now, "everyone" tells you that you should not watch the stock price of your company daily. I even said that to all my employees. It is fruitless, and you can't sell the stock anyway. As I mentioned, selling was tightly regulated until after the six-month holding period, and even then, it was tightly regulated to selling within certain windows. The RealReal management team always said that they were in it for the long game and the daily swings of the stock were irrelevant. And yet every executive had the stock price flashing on their phone or their computer or both. And the swings would drive them to distraction. I can honestly say I was in it for the long game, and yet the daily swings also drove me to distraction, too.

Selling is still restricted to open windows post the six-month lock-up period if you are in the company. Consequently, most early investors who were on the board pre-public made plans to exit the board quickly so they could sell without those restrictions. One investor never exited the board and consequently appeared not to have sold any of his stock. This person would call me weekly asking me what was going on. This investor was the last institutional investor prior to the company going public. After his firm invested, he joined the board about one year before we went public.

This person would reach out to me when the stock moved two to three dollars downward when the company was in its quiet period, meaning no new financial information was public. There was not an identifiable reason why the stock moved when there were no public announcements, and if an investor was selling a large amount of stock, we did not have that information. Stock sales are not transparent to the company. I should have realized something was going on with him. I really should have taken note. It did appear to me that he was under pressure from his own fund as The RealReal stock moved downward and erased gains on his investment. From my vantage point, it appeared he made a mistake by not selling stock. There would be a future price to pay.

The RealReal had investors since 2011. The first made small investments ranging from $25,000 to $100,000. Then venture capital investments into the millions started in 2012. Every lead venture capital investor tends to get a board seat or at least a board observer role.

Observers may talk at board meetings but not vote. There is no such thing as a silent partner or someone just observing, in any scenario. The RealReal didn't have silent partners—we had investors, and those investors comprised the board. These investors, especially Series A, B, and C investors, had their money in the company a long time without a payout. Remember, everyone answers to someone. These investors had investors. And companies they invest in either go public, get sold, or pay off those investors through future earnings. Venture capital outcomes are usually generated by the sale of the company and secondarily by the company going public. Most venture capital funds have a ten-plus-year life, which means their funds can show great returns when just a few companies hit. It also means that it takes a long time for early stage companies to deliver a significant return. This is a long explanation to let you know that almost every one of my board members would be exiting the board in the next six to twelve months. In order to sell their stock and receive the return on their investment, they had to vacate their seats on the board. This allowed them to avoid selling in the "open window" period, which is pre-determined in writing to the SEC and lasts for a short period of time each quarter. After a short waiting period and resigning from the board, the earliest investors were free to sell opportunistically.

Smart investors do exit boards and do what they do best—sell the stock and get great returns for their investors. It is not a personal decision. Keep this in mind. As expected, within nine months of going public, all the original Silicon Valley tech investors and Mike Kumin had exited from The RealReal board. The only holdover from our pre-IPO board was the guy whose money was the last money into the company.

We needed new board members, but I made some major mistakes in recommending replacements. The biggest mistake I made was that

I did not recommend board members with shared values. Recall that an ideal start-up employee most likely didn't come from a corporate environment with a hierarchical mindset. For some reason, I didn't use the same criteria when I recommended new board members. I recommended people who had developed a skill set in their functional area. But they were all from a corporate environment and had a fixed hierarchical mindset. Further, none of the new board members I recommended had been in a fast growing, technology based, innovative company. They had no idea what type of person thrived in that environment, and they had never experienced the perils, pitfalls and magical success of those types of companies. The new board members were from disparate industries, but all corporate women. The mixture could and did become toxic.

You know by now that I am well over fifty. I thrive when I lead collaborative, fast-moving, high-growth companies that bend toward a meritocracy. I left the corporate world at the age of twenty-five and joined an early stage technology company because I didn't want to be among the people I saw above me. Even at that young age, I knew I wouldn't be great at playing the political game. Those people aren't and weren't my people.

Women had and still have a hard time with career advancement within corporations. The hard data supports this, and so does the anecdotal information. The women who are fifty now started working when sexual harassment laws were just being introduced. I doubt any human resource executive was worried about wage equality for the same position. In fact, it took one woman, Lilly Ledbetter, and her determination to make sure what happened to her in her corporate job didn't happen to other women. She worked tirelessly to pass the Lilly Ledbetter Fair Pay Act of 2009 to ensure people doing the same job would be paid the same wages. Lilly never benefited from that new law and could not recover lost wages because laws on the books limited the time period for such claims.

Further, there were few executive women above them or anywhere, so they had no role models. They had to fight hard to succeed in a corporate environment. Since that world bends heavily toward the political, they learned how to operate within those rules. Typically, there wasn't room for more than one woman at the top. Supporting other women who may compete with them was not something they excelled at. This has since been given a name: *code switching*. Code switching means taking on unnatural but rewarded behaviors to succeed. If you code switch long enough, you become that person. So, there are reasons some women don't support other women.

This all leads to my very broad generalization: Older corporate women can be pretty nasty to other women. I have heard too many stories from other women to know that what I experienced wasn't isolated. The key takeaway for anyone considering a board member: It is best to recommend board members with shared values, shared work experiences, and great functional experience. Another lesson I learned the hard way.

As a public company, The RealReal would be reporting financial results for the second quarter, Q2 2019, the second week of September. Before we reported our financial results, several interesting things happened rapid fire from the end of August into early September 2019. They seemed tied to each other when they were happening and still do upon reflection.

First, a film crew posing as reporters showed up at our West Hollywood store. Two fake reporters were shoving microphones in customers' faces as they left the store. They were aggressive and disruptive. The person in charge of all the retail stores happened to be at the store that day. He called Rati, and Rati called me. We both told him to call the police. But he tried something even better first: He asked them if they had a permit to film on the street and told them the police had been called. And the police would arrive quickly since their station was close to the store. The fake reporters did not have a permit to film. The retail head then said he would have to confiscate their equipment, which of course he had no right to do, but it was a good bluff and it worked. The fake reporters left quickly. They said they were hired by a research company, and they didn't want any trouble. Research company my ass.

The very same day, and this went on for over seven working days, police showed up at our luxury consignment offices asking for the legal pawnshop documentation. We had the documentation back at corporate, not in the individual facilities. One by one across the United States, the luxury consignment offices were closed by the police until our corporate lawyers could provide the appropriate documentation.

Let's set the scene here. You have a beautiful office with serene music playing. It is staffed by a receptionist. The people working in the offices are gemologists. There is a large safe bolted to the floor somewhere in the small office. Now the police barge in—some in full riot gear—demand to see the paperwork, and state that this facility has been reported as a pawnshop operating outside of the law. Frantic calls were made to the corporate general counsel, to Rati, to me, whoever would pick up the phone. The offices were forced to close immediately. The consignors having their meetings were escorted out. This created extreme unease for the employees, and we certainly lost business during the days we were closed.

The RealReal's corporate lawyer spent the next day or two in conversations with local police officers, sending the appropriate paperwork to them so the offices could reopen.

All the while, someone was sitting back thinking about their little plan and how it disrupted The RealReal. Maybe they were thinking about their bonus or their success fee. They probably got bonus points if they had been able to place stories with major publications like the *Wall Street Journal* or the *New York Times*, or even Page Six of the *New York Post* about how The RealReal operates illegally. And this same person or group of people probably was getting excited about putting this story in their investor newsletter.

Except The RealReal did not operate illegally and had the paperwork.

I immediately reached out to my board of directors. They recommended hiring a specialty public relations firm to put strategies in place to offset these actions. The board had limited experience with public companies and had never seen anything like we were experiencing. We were playing defense here and needed experience to maneuver through this nightmare. Defense is never the best tactic, but we had to. We hired Sard Verbinnen and Co to help us with damage control after we had the raids on the luxury consignment offices. We had to bring them up to speed quickly because we knew something else was brewing due to what was happening at the Secaucus facility.

A reporter with a small camera crew had been literally popping out of the bushes at our Secaucus facility to harass The RealReal employees as they ate lunch or left the facility. The reporter gave his card to a couple of employees. One of those cards ended up being texted to The RealReal's head of communication. We also had been reading the posts of one of our employees, who was exuberantly writing about being picked up by limo and having her hair and makeup done for her television appearance. This young woman was a receiver at The RealReal. She was on and off probation due to her poor performance. I guess she must have been bragging because one of her coworkers had alerted people back at corporate about her postings. The reporter was from CNBC, the studio shots posted by the employee were in a professional television studio.

The day before we reported our financial results, CNBC decided to publish this exposé on The RealReal. I am using the word *exposé* with charity. It was a hit job. We were asked to comment on the story the night before the story aired, but we were not allowed to understand the angle of the story. It may seem odd, since the story was already written, but this is how some reporters work. They have their point of view, and they do not want to alter the story with the facts if the facts don't support their premise. We were in that situation, and we knew it. Blindly commenting does not serve the company when this happens. We did not want to comment without reading or seeing the story. What was clear to us was the timing of this exposé seemed planned to do maximum harm.

CNBC reported that The RealReal sells fakes. As I recall, they had three people on record. The first was the employee who was posting about the limo ride and the hair and makeup. She said that she was supposed to inspect every item, but she didn't, and they were all on quotas and the quotas were too high. The second person, an older woman, was angry because we had shipped her the wrong item—which, by the way, was authentic—and she said something like, "I'd like to give Julie Wainwright a piece of mind." I would have happily called her and told her she could just return the scarf at our cost and give her a $25 shopping credit for her inconvenience.

The last person featured was once a luxury salesperson who had left the company and went to work for a competitor. She had taken The RealReal's customer base with her. This action was in direct violation of the California Uniform Trade Secrets Act. So, we sued the company she went to work for. The filmmakers flashed the lawsuit up and then had her saying something like she never authenticated items, and she never saw anyone do it at the warehouse. First, luxury sales managers didn't have to authenticate. In fact, it would put them in a very awkward position with their customers if they said they couldn't take an item because it was fake. Second, she didn't see anyone authenticate any item because she shipped her things to the operations centers, and she didn't work there. The lawsuit was settled by her new employer.

CNBC and its collaborators achieved a result that the other actions had not. We announced our financial results from our first public quarter and we had overdelivered on expectations. That should have been viewed as good news. The positive financial results versus the plan didn't make a positive difference in the stock price. In fact, the stock closed lower. Again, that very same day we announced our financial performance and the CNBC story aired, a newsletter company writing for the short-selling, conspiracy-loving side of the market had reported that we called our authenticators, copywriters. We did call the first level of authenticators copywriters because they wrote copy and authenticated items. We never gave the title of our copywriters a second thought. But clearly, someone at the newsletter for short sellers thought that was a big story. We did eventually call them authenticators, and not copywriters, because machine learning and artificial intelligence took over most of the copywriting as the company matured.

What was going on here? Was CNBC a useful tool for one of The RealReal's adversaries? I'll never know for sure. But when something like this happens, an old maxim is helpful: Follow the money. Who had money to lose or gain? Chanel, for one, was quite vocal about its displeasure with The RealReal. And I felt that Chanel had a history of actively trying to stop the company from succeeding. But maybe it was Tiffany, because a few weeks later there was an incident with a Tiffany item. A fake piece of Tiffany jewelry was submitted to The RealReal by mail. This person, oddly enough, had the same name as the author of the copywriter/authenticator story in the short-seller newsletter.

And, that person then used the Miami police department address as their home address. Was his name a coincidence? Probably not. Was Tiffany underwriting the short seller's newsletter and the fake Tiffany item experiment? Maybe. Tiffany used the same law firm as Chanel. Were those two colluding against The RealReal? Actually, it could have been any of the large brands, really. I know the short sellers benefited. And it wouldn't have surprised me if some executive somewhere sent out a gleeful memo when the CNBC piece aired. Somebody and some entities were happy. I was not.

After many discussions, the consensus from our public relations firm and internal team was we needed to rebut the CNBC story. An interview was set up with me to go on Jim Cramer's CNBC show *Mad Money*. But I wanted to meet the head of CNBC first. We all wanted to understand the motive behind the story.

Our head of communications set up an in-person meeting with Dan Colarusso, the senior vice president of CNBC business news, a few hours before my appearance on Cramer's show.

We met in his office. There was an immediate air of apprehensiveness and a pinch of hostility in the room. We brought the hostility. Our head of communications pointed out all the inaccuracies in the reporting. She had a sternness in her voice that I had never heard before. Dan started the meeting with what seemed like a forced grin on his face, then he turned ashen, then he got his other reporters on the speakerphone. I asked him who he was serving by this story. A brand, many brands, short sellers? He wasn't answering our questions directly or at all. I was seething by then, and it showed. He only said we cater to everyone. I kept asking him questions. I generally tend to be oddly clearheaded in my anger. And this was one of those moments. I was very angry and rational. He said nothing. It felt like he dialed his reporters into our meeting to make himself feel better, and maybe afterward so he could commiserate with them over the two angry women he had in his office.

We kept asking him whose pocket they were in and why. He never answered us. The RealReal was the only company that authenticated preowned luxury goods on a mass scale. We all knew that many of the luxury brands considered The RealReal a threat. Maybe it was about sex and money, not just money. It certainly was not about ethical and groundbreaking reporting.

After we left Dan's office, I had a few minutes to get my hair and makeup refreshed before I was scheduled for Jim Cramer's show. I replaced my anger with the calm headspace that I needed for the show. My goal was to talk to Jim about the facts of how The RealReal authenticates items and give data points about the large number of goods processed and the accuracy rate of our authentication. The clip is still on YouTube. At the time, I thought I did well, and I can be hard on myself. After the interview, he walked me part of the way off the stage. He covered his mike after the interview and said his wife loves The RealReal. So, there's that.

I had two CNBC on-air reporters call me and apologize, saying CNBC had never done anything like this before. Well, they had just done it. An apology seemed pointless but was still appreciated. Sadly, the damage was done. Consequently, I and my CFO had to answer to our investors.

The axiom "There is no such thing as bad press" must have originated from the public relations industry itself. Bad press does hurt companies. Retractions and rebuttals are for the history books and help support companies and individuals in lawsuits, but they are seldom noticed.

Sometime before 2019 ended, Chanel sued The RealReal. A year or so later, The RealReal countersued. Both lawsuits are ongoing as I write this.

Business had to go on. I was worried that the negative press would impact our current and future luxury brand deals. Allison and I were also working on a deal with Gucci, and we were finalizing the contract with Burberry, hoping to launch both in early 2020. Gucci was still interested in a meeting, and Allison and I were asked to meet Marco Bizzarri in Detroit at the Shinola Hotel.

Marco and I sat across from each other in a private dining space in the hotel. There were four other Gucci executives with him.

"Remember that night you monopolized me?" he said, and I thought, *What a perfect opener.*

"At the *Vanity Fair* dinner? Yes, of course. Was it that painful?"

"Not really."

And then we started discussions about how we could work together in a way that was unique to the Gucci brand. The meeting lasted over an hour. No one mentioned the bad press The RealReal had gotten on CNBC just a few months before. Maybe the executives at Gucci had missed the news. I was certainly hoping they had.

I was looking forward to the end of 2019. It was a year of extreme highs, achieved lifetime goals, exuberant feelings of taking the public company—and then there were the extreme lows. That is the life an entrepreneur signs up for, but even with that lens, it felt extreme. And the man I was dating and I had parted ways. Our ending started with him wanting to discuss the impending differences in our net worth and me being confused by that discussion because I hadn't sold one share of stock. He then told me he never wanted to get married again, to which I replied, "Did I ask you to marry me?" He was confused by that and had to admit I had never brought it up. In any case, we were done. And that was sad because he was good company, but neither of us were each other's big love.

I would have tried harder if I had thought he was a big love. I did really care for him, and I will always cherish the moments we had together. Somewhere in my heart, I still thought that it was possible to find true love, not just a good companion. I knew it felt like a sentiment a woman in her early twenties would harbor, but I couldn't shake the feeling that there could have been something more than what the two of us had, someone who moved my soul. On the business side, a key executive said he was going to resign in the next nine to twelve months for personal reasons. I considered this resignation a positive one. Now we could hire an executive with deep public company experience. I needed that person by my side.

Chapter 13

You Can Stop the Growth

There is a British saying that is particularly charming: *tickety-boo*, meaning "in good order," and it was applicable as The RealReal headed into 2020. At The RealReal everything was tickety-boo in January 2020. We were on a solid path of growth with profitability within eighteen months. We had ended 2019 strong and would be able to report a very good fourth quarter when we announced our financial results in late February.

The intentional disruption of the business caused by the luxury consignment police raids and fake reporters, the short seller newsletter stories, and the impact of the CNBC reporting had died down. Even though the CNBC reporting had a negative impact on our stock and we had to answer to it on the analyst calls, it never hurt the consumer demand for our products. It did have a longer impact on the stock price, though.

Still, there was a general feeling in the office that we could all take a breath and focus on delivering results. People returned from the holiday break in good spirits. We were preparing to open a store on Post Street on San Francisco's Union Square. It was exciting to have a store in the same city as our corporate headquarters. The store opened on March 10, 2020. Emily Chang of Bloomberg TV covered the opening. London Breed, the mayor of San Francisco, stopped by to cut the ribbon with me and shopped a little. The store looked amazing. It was one of the most beautiful stores we had. It had two major ways to enter it. The front door was on Post Street, and the backdoor opened to the Maiden Lane alleyway. Maiden Lane is a pedestrian-only area that can be beautiful and relaxing when Union Square is bustling. Chanel, Gucci, Cartier, and Hermès all had doors that opened to this back alley.

The executives from the corporate office were at the store opening, something many had never experienced. It was a good beginning and a proud moment for all who had worked so hard to build the company. Something about having this store in the same city as the corporate office made it even more important. This was a showcase store for The RealReal and one that would allow us to run merchandising and marketing tests that could possibly be expanded to the other stores. A big party was planned for our consignors in a week at the store. The invitations had been sent out. Then there was some news that made us reconsider the party.

A new virus was being reported in the Bay Area. COVID-19 was starting to get some news coverage, and it sounded like a terrible flu that was easily communicable. Given the reported COVID concerns, we postponed our opening-night party. No one could imagine what happened next. On March 17, 2020, San Francisco issued a mandatory stay-at-home order, which was expected to lift on April 7, 2020. I watched Governor Newsom's press conference and then reread Mayor Breed's mandate, the stay-at-home order. It was clear to me that they had no idea what we were facing. I never believed the two-week notice. It didn't make sense to me.

I pulled my management team together before we all vacated the offices. Here is pretty much what I told them: "First, the two-week stay-at-home order appears to be made-up. Let's not count on it. What we need to do is assume that this will go on longer. We need to have a plan in place that if it is not lifted in two weeks, we will have to make some drastic changes. The brick-and-mortar employees will have to be furloughed. The operation center employees in California will have to be furloughed, too. Any other support teams that will need to be put on furlough? This may be a time to lay off some people, too. What's going on with New Jersey? Any news? Can we get the mayor of Perth Amboy on the phone? Ideally that operations center can stay open." I remember the head of human relations saying that was a lot to consider. I said we could talk about it tomorrow, but we needed to be ready for the furlough and layoffs if the two weeks were extended.

Then we left and agreed to meet daily at 9 a.m. via Zoom. The warehouse in Brisbane was closed. New Jersey hadn't issued the same mandate yet, so our warehouses in Perth Amboy and Secaucus were still operating, which was good. What was troubling was the halt to our ability to acquire products. The RealReal is not a self-posting site, meaning a person cannot list their own items on the site. This was a RealReal strategic design choice. I wanted the company to set the standards for brand, condition, and authenticity. The primary method of product acquisition was home visits, with store drop-offs second. Clearly that wasn't going to be able to happen. By the end of March, all retail stores in New York City were closed—our largest market was closed completely. We had limited to no ability to pick up goods.

New Jersey allowed us to operate at a limited capacity. So we could do some processing in our Perth Amboy and Secaucus facilities. But about 40 percent of all our inventory was in Brisbane, California. This was grim.

Revenue had dropped off quickly. We ended February 2020 with revenue up 40 percent versus the previous year. The second half of March had dropped to negative 40 percent in revenue versus the previous year. Our business had an 80-point swing in two weeks. It felt terrifying. The only consolation was that we were all going through it together. And the only thing to do was to plan and execute where we could. We had to take it day by day. And every day at 9 a.m. and again at 5 p.m., the executive team at The RealReal would meet to discuss state by state closures, what was happening with customer service and demand, product acquisition, and employee attitude. We also had a daily COVID check.

By early April, it appeared that we could continue to operate in our New Jersey facilities at a limited capacity. We needed to get back in our operations center in Brisbane and transfer the inventory from Brisbane to New Jersey. Beyond getting the new product on the website, we needed to process people's returns. A small team of people went into the warehouse to scope the job. Within a few hours a law enforcement officer, I believe it was the sheriff, pounded on the door and asked to enter the building. The Brisbane facility was 250,000 square feet. There were seven people in the building including a security guard at the time. The policeman ordered them to vacate the premises and promised he would put his own lock on our doors if any employee tried to get into the facility again. Business arguments fell on deaf ears. This man had newly expanded authority, and he was going to use it. This incident resulted in a series of discussions with the town of Brisbane's lawyer and any politician within San Mateo County who would talk to us. It took weeks of discussions. No one moved off their position.

In late April/early May, we were finally able to have a limited staff in the Brisbane facility to move the product from Brisbane to New Jersey. The police were supervising to make sure that we were complying with people per square foot and COVID precautions in our facility. It seemed like overreach and extremely authoritarian, and it was. Still, we had to abide by the laws.

In the meantime, I was interviewing for a new general counsel for The RealReal. We had an interim lawyer working with us, as our previous lawyer had resigned due to significant health and family problems. We had narrowed the candidate field prior to COVID closures, and the finalist, Todd Suko, lived about three miles from me. We decided to go on a walking interview around the town of Tiburon. It was Todd, me, and some wild turkeys roaming the streets that early morning. COVID made strange bedfellows. My phone rang during our walk. It was the mayor of Perth Amboy. I'd been trying to reach her, so I had to take the call in the middle of our walking interview. I leaned against the doorway of a closed restaurant while Todd stood by.

"Julie, we have had many complaints about the conditions in the Perth Amboy warehouse."

"What specifically?"

"Overcrowding. No masks required."

"As you know, we have 500,000 square feet of space there. We are running two shifts now with only one hundred people per shift. Prior to COVID, we had four hundred plus workers in that space. And masks are mandatory. We provide them. We also have the area sanitized twice a day."

"We are getting an inordinate number of calls stating otherwise."

"You are free to tour the warehouse anytime. Just let me know five minutes before you arrive so I can let the floor managers know. I am curious, though, were the calls from local numbers? As you know, most of our employees are local."

"Give me a minute to check." She put me on hold. I looked at Todd and asked, "Are you hearing any of this?"

"At least your side of it, yes," he replied.

The mayor came back on the line. "Most of the calls appear to be coming from Connecticut numbers."

"How about that. Probably a short-seller scheme."

"What?"

"We have had significant business interruptions since we went public. Hard to know the exact source, could be people who make their money on shorting a stock. This feels like that."

"I see."

"Feel free to visit. You will see what is happening. And, if there are any issues that you identify, we will address them."

Despite having a very odd interview, Todd took the job. The mayor did send some people to inspect the operations center. There were no complaints going forward. I was happy that I had taken the time to know the mayor prior to her phone call. She had my cell and vice versa. We had developed a level of trust during our lunch at the official opening of the Perth Amboy operations center. She knew she could always reach out. Further, we had asked for her office's help in recruiting for the hundreds of jobs we had open when the facility began operating fully. I had tried to meet the mayor of Brisbane when we were moving there. The mayor made it clear she did not want a fully operating warehouse in her town. She was worried about traffic. She saw no value in bringing jobs to the Brisbane area. Maybe she didn't care because the increased tax revenue and local business revenue associated with more jobs in Brisbane went to the County of San Mateo, not the local city. This appears to be a misalignment of incentives. The net result:

Brisbane's law enforcement wanted to keep us locked out, and Perth Amboy's team wanted to keep us operating as long as we were doing so safely.

Then a *New York Times* article was published that cited that The RealReal was still operating in New Jersey, and it was troubling for employees, putting them at risk. The reporter who wrote the article had been reaching out to anyone who would talk to her across many operating warehouses. One employee working in Secaucus did talk and express her distress at having to work during COVID. I wrote a long response to the *New York Times* reporter. My letter was never published. We terminated the employee.

Here's the sad thing: At the beginning of April 2020, we offered all employees—those that were not laid off or furloughed with the retail team—three options. First, they could stay on as an employee, but their hours would be cut because of mandated restrictions on the number of people in a confined area. Second, they could be furloughed and collect unemployment from the government, and the company would pay their health benefits for three months. And third, they could be laid off and collect unemployment and pay their own benefits. It was the employee's choice. The US government was paying more per hour than our starting wage, which for perspective was almost two times more than the required New Jersey minimum wage. Economically, it made sense for people to ask to be laid off if they were covered under someone else's health-care plan.

All employers who had hourly employees were in the same situation. The government was paying people more money to stay home than an employer could afford to pay them to work. I understand the motivation, but this wasn't a great solution at the beginning of COVID. It became a serious problem as workplace restrictions were lifted. Both the Trump and Biden administrations created this problem.

The person who spoke to the *New York Times* that day made a choice that resulted in her termination, which meant she had no ability to collect unemployment and had to pay her own health insurance. That made me sad for her. She clearly made a bad decision. How did we know she talked to the reporter? She used her work laptop for all communication. The RealReal, like other companies, monitors work devices.

Demand for products on The RealReal site started to pick up again in May 2020. High-value handbags and jewelry were increasingly in demand. Designer shoes were also in high demand, which was a head scratcher. Who was wearing shoes? This may have been a bright moment in an otherwise horrible situation except that we had no ability to pick up products. Quite a few customers outside of the NYC area were calling us for pickups. Given our limited experience with overly zealous law enforcement, we decided to use plain white vans to pick up product curbside. The RealReal had a fleet of branded vans in use by 2020. Those were kept at the warehouse.

There were three areas of the country where it felt like COVID never happened: Newport Beach, California; Florida; and Arizona. Product began to trickle in. The sales team were responding for requests for pick-ups. The stealth vans were helping in the pick-ups. All product was sent to New Jersey. Still, we had a huge product supply deficit. In general, The RealReal had over fifteen weeks of inventory on hand before COVID. Two months into COVID and we were down to under six weeks of inventory. We had to do something. We needed to buy some product or risk losing our customer base. As I mentioned before, we have always had some vendor product on the site. With all stores closed (except in the abovementioned areas), vendors wanted to sell to any online company. So, we started buying product to partially fill the demand gap.

Vendor product wasn't usually desirable, especially if it was overstock. The beauty of resale, simply stated, is: If it sold once, it will sell again. Overstock didn't sell the first time and when we experimented with it on the site early on, it didn't sell the second time on our site. However, most of the vendor product that reached our site during COVID didn't have an opportunity to sell anywhere because of store closures. The downside of vendor product was that the margins at 35 percent were not as healthy as the product margins on consignment. You know what the real downside was? Having empty shelves. Last time I checked the math, 35 percent times 0 was 0. We were facing zero and had to take the margin hit temporarily.

Rati had operations reporting to her right after we went public. She now had to find ways to process products with safety and law enforcement in mind. She creatively found ways to do this in the stores and in our corporate office in San Francisco when the restrictions loosened a little, but retail stores still could not open.

Given the issues in Brisbane during COVID, which just compounded our challenges in general in running an operations center in the state of California, we all worked to move our operations out of the state of California sooner than we had planned. We needed a bigger space than the one we were in prior to COVID. As I mentioned earlier, for planning purposes to accommodate our growth, we had started looking for expansion space in Arizona and Texas before COVID hit. The unpredictability of the Texas power grid combined with some archaic pawnshop laws that may or may not have applied to our operations center pushed us toward Phoenix, Arizona. Our Brisbane, California, landlord, Prologis, owned a building in Phoenix and said it would work with us to expedite our move. Prior to our decision to move out of California, I had met with local San Mateo County and California state officials to see if there were any incentives that could be offered to keep us in the state. Arizona and Texas were both offering incentives. The answer from California was a flat-out no. Just getting to the correct person in California was hard and exhausting. The answer was not a surprise.

Accelerating the move would lessen the risk of operational COVID closures and other issues that came with running an operations center in a state that was not employer friendly. The move also had inherent risk—transferring the skills from one workforce to another. We made Brisbane employees in good standing offers to join the team in Phoenix and even offered to pay for their trip to visit the area. About 50 out of 350 made the decision to move with us. A few even put a down payment on a home there, something they could not do in California. We kept their pay the same.

Since we all lived through COVID, we all experienced the emotional and mental stress of this time. Then came George Floyd's murder on May 25, 2020. The horror of what happened to him reverberated throughout our company. The RealReal employed more women than men and more minorities than any company I have ever run. Our Black employees were angry and deeply saddened. My notes and conversations to the employees were not enough. I had anger directed toward me.

I needed to understand the emotions they were going through as best as I could. One of my best friends for thirty years is an African American woman, and we had never talked about discrimination before. Ever. And she is a mom to a son and daughter. She has a Black husband. She opened my eyes and talked freely. Her husband works with companies and government agencies to discuss what it is like to be Black in the US with the goal of educating people for positive change. I asked him to hold a series of meetings with the management team. We all had our eyes opened. We started a series of talks and brought in more experts to educate us all. There were two Indian American executives on my team. Both shared that they had felt discriminated against outside of The RealReal. It was clear an African American had a different level of difficulty to deal with daily than what they had experienced. We set up special groups to encourage conversation. These were baby steps to complex issues.

By May, most of our stores had opened to limited capacity. Long lines formed down the block as shoppers slowly came back and waited patiently for one person to leave so another could go in the store. Then the riots and the looting started. The RealReal store on Melrose Avenue in West Hollywood was seriously damaged on the men's side. It felt like an inside job because they pried open the backdoor and went straight to where the most valuable items were usually kept. Since we have cameras everywhere and there was a direct feed of the security cameras in my desk area, I watched the store being destroyed. The police watched, too. They were outside the store and completely outnumbered. They didn't attempt to restrain the looters. Down the street, another store was set on fire.

We had to take a drastic next step. All stores were boarded up after that and remained so for months. Once the looting and rioting stopped, the nighttime mob robbing started. Security measures got tighter. Morale slipped lower. We just kept adding more security, repairing the store fixtures, replacing the broken windows, restocking the shelves, and attempting to calm people down. It felt like a fruitless effort. The police were not equipped to deal with this kind of theft because the robberies happened so quickly, and they were always outnumbered by the masses of people involved in the theft. It always took less than three minutes for the thieves to clean out the store. There were usually thirty-five to forty of them pouring through the broken door or window and rushing out with their loot to the waiting cars.

The security videos were sickening. People pouring in, wearing hood- ies and masks, destroying displays, throwing fixtures to the ground, grabbing as much as they could carry as they rushed out the door. It is terrible seeing something people have built with great intentions destroyed so quickly.

About half of The RealReal employees lived in the New York/New Jersey area. I traveled back east as soon as I could to see the teams at the operations centers, the Midtown offices, and the sales team. That was sometime in late September 2020. People's spirits were flat at best. Next stop was Chicago. We opened a store in downtown Chicago in Octo- ber 2020. That was a miraculous feat for all involved. When I walked into it, it made me cry because I could only imagine what it took to make this happen. And then I wondered how quickly we would have to board it up. That came within days of its opening.

As things were easing somewhat in the operations department and consignment was starting to come in, still significantly below the year before, other dramas were happening with my executive team. Fredrik Björk, our CTO, had decided to move his family back home. He wanted to stay with the company and work from home. Working from home was not a problem except when your home is in Sweden. He and his wife wanted his kids back in school. They didn't want to live in San Francisco any further and had rented homes across the state of Califor- nia when restrictions eased. Still unhappy, he wanted to go home and be close to his family in Sweden. We didn't call him Fredrik of Sweden for nothing. He gave me plenty of notice, but that was still a loss.

And a top executive had figuratively put a gun to my head, demanding they be promoted to expand their span of control and run another department, otherwise they would resign. Normally I would have said no, and if you want to, resign. I didn't say that this time. This person caught me at a weak moment. Needless to say, that didn't work out well for that person or for the company. This person is a brilliant executive in their field. They could not run both departments. So, this person had to be terminated. That meant that I needed to fill a couple of executive roles. One of the new hires did not work out for many reasons, including that they seemed more concerned about their personal brand than delivering results.

Then an executive who had resigned said they wanted to stay. This executive said they wanted to be part of the team that drove the company to profitability. When an executive resigns, a lot of actions are put in place to fill their position. The board is notified immediately. Some key executives are notified. In this case, I was down the road of filling the soon-to-be vacant position. Now it was up to me to convince this person to leave. It seemed like this person had other plans.

While I was trying to get this person to honor their prior resignation so we could have a smooth transition, this person was apparently working against me with a couple of the executives. I didn't think I'd be in my own *Game of Thrones*, but I was. This executive couldn't get anyone except the newbies to join the rebellion. When that situation bubbled up to me, the person had to leave on the company's terms. The newbies washed out less than a year later. Both were wrong for the position in a public company with over $1 billion in revenue (well, $1 billion in 2019).

Neither had ever had the top job in a public company. Having a big, first-string job in a public company is different from playing second or third string in a similar-size company. Top executives have no place to hide. They must be ready for the accountability and responsibility of their recommendations and actions. They don't have their boss to protect them, so the position is exponentially harder and certainly there is more pressure. Ambition is no substitute for talent, maturity, and experience. One of our new executive employees asked for the position of COO before they had even proven themselves in the job they were hired to do. Not a great strategy for any employee.

Sometimes people are ready, and they can step up. These people have tremendous capacity, and if you have someone like this in your organization, put an inordinate amount of time into them. The payback will be substantial. They put in the work and really understand how to drive success and hire well. Rati is a great example. I kept giving her more, and she kept mastering what she was given.

As 2020 inched to a close, we had managed to nearly match the revenue from 2019. We were about 5 percent below 2019. Some of the analysts and apparently some of my own board members had a hard time understanding why we weren't growing like the self-posting sites at the time. Companies like Poshmark, the self-posting resale site were doing fine. The RealReal was clawing itself out of a deep hole.

And, unbeknownst to me, a board member, or maybe a couple of board members, were building a case against me. I believe that this was led by the person who apparently had not sold his shares, although I cannot be sure. But it is almost always about the money, and that person had not gotten a good return on his investment. Having executive turmoil did not help my case, I am sure. Most of the executives had been with the company for more than seven years. They had made some money. COVID was a breaking point for many of them. Three exited during the COVID period. To be fair, I did make some bad hires. I misfired on a couple of executives during this time. Having said that, the board was involved in the interviewing process. One board member was very enthusiastic about one of the potential executive hires. He was wrong and so was I. Ultimately, unless the board is running the company, the CEO is the decision-maker, and the responsibility rests with that person.

The Chicago store had launched, the Phoenix operations center move was underway, and the management team was in high drama. Every year had closed with highs and lows. This one closed with lows and thankfulness. We were all thankful that only one employee had lost their life during the year. He was in his twenties. It was an illness, but it was not COVID related. It was still a loss. He was the second person who had lost their life since The RealReal's formation. The first young man was the victim of a hit-and-run in New York City.

It was a scary year. I was glad it was over.

Chapter 14

Are We Done with That Yet?

The 2020 nervousness rolled into 2021, and so did the employee fatigue. This was a big year for The RealReal, though. It was our tenth birthday. Ten years! Rati had been with me since day one. She was so young then, at least in my mind. And now she was almost forty, and she was married and had two children. She kept growing and taking on more responsibilities. On our tenth anniversary, she told me her parents wanted to put more money in the company in the earliest days when we really needed it. She advised them not to do it. Of course, my reaction was a loud "What?" And then I burst into laughter. I think that moment was captured in my favorite ten-year celebration photo of us. She had waited ten years to tell me that. Timing is everything. She had told me a while before that her father had a meeting with her early on to discuss how she should work with me, which included a message that she needed to work hard, that this was an opportunity.

Rachel Vaisman had also joined the company early. She was the NYC sales director, the operations manager, the keep-the-lights-on person when our accounting department forgot to pay the electric bill. Literally, she kept the lights on by paying off the guy who came to turn off the electricity. She gave him twenty dollars and asked him to give her two days to get all outstanding bills paid. He said okay, and the bills were paid. Money talks.

Here's the amazing thing about a start-up that works and goes into accelerated growth: Everyone is given the opportunity to grow. If an employee was accountable, smart, a proactive problem-solver, and played well with others, the spirit at The RealReal was "come on, take more." Promoting from within is the best course for most companies. It certainly worked well for The RealReal. As a founder and CEO, it is incredibly gratifying for me to see people grow professionally. It is an honor to witness. I saw it time and time again. There were times I believed in people more than they believed in themselves. I know people did things they didn't think were possible. And they made more money than they thought they would.

The ten-year anniversary mark was energizing for us. Coming out of such a tough time and still experiencing the long tail of COVID, it allowed us a moment to reflect on the entire ten years of fun, growth, and impact The RealReal had on the fashion industry. I took a moment to savor that. The idea for the business had come to me when I was facing one of the biggest challenges of my life professionally and financially. Once I had the idea, the research showed me it was a big opportunity that had not been realized. Then I got lucky in meeting Rati Sahi, now Rati Sahi Levesque after her marriage, the first employee and the one who would be my right-hand person. I also got lucky that her dad told her to embrace the opportunity. The venture capital investors were also amazing and world class. Even though we had our moments in board meetings, they always came through. Then we had executed beautifully for the most part. The key for the demand of the business was changing the perception of resale. The RealReal had done that. The key for the supply side of the business was service. We had created a service business that did not exist before The RealReal. The key to longevity was to build a competitive moat and create a profitable business. The moat was built. The profitability had to come next.

I also took stock of The RealReal venture capitalists who financed the company, offered guidance, and helped at every turn. The board members who made a difference were the original team of Maha Ibrahim, Mathias Schilling, Keval Desai, Cynthia Ringo, and Mike Kumin. Dana Settle, an active board observer, worked as hard as the board members to make the business work. Each one made significant contributions at various stages of the company. Most important, they kept the company financed and helped bring in talent. Each person brought something slightly different to the table.

Maha was deep in the financials and also a The RealReal user. She worked with us on the unit economics and the user experience. Mathias was also deep into the financials and cohort analysis. He probably did the most in extending our network for future financing. Keval took the long view when building companies and had perspectives that challenged us all to think bigger while executing daily. Cynthia's firm, DBL, was the most unique venture firm, and its mission and ours were aligned. She introduced us to the Ellen MacArthur Foundation, which ultimately led to us being able to quantify the positive impact of consigning. Then there was Mike, the private equity guy. He elevated all conversations around the table. His perspective was also a long view of the company, and he worked on the strategic and tactical all the time. Last, Dana Settle lent us members of her team to workshop the business with us, and she was always thinking of creative ways to keep the company financed.

Now that doesn't mean it was all fun and games around the board-room table. We had many tough conversations. The growth of The RealReal caused strains on the infrastructure, the management team, and most of all, our need for capital. The RealReal was and is a business of scale, and we were burning a lot of money as we scaled the company.

There was one tense moment that stands out and is worth discussing because it underscores the collaborative nature of these investors. This happened before Mike Kumin joined the board.

The investors, two in particular, wanted to discuss getting to profitability early, closer to year six when the company was still in its high-growth mode. I knew that if we stopped investing in our infrastructure and brand building, we would have a zombie company that would ultimately fail. In the early days, we were meeting every month. So, this conversation was a continuous one. I was adamant about not slowing the growth. During this time, *Harvard Business Review* published a study of our great internal debate. The study concluded that both male and female venture capitalists speak completely differently to women and men CEOs. Men are asked questions about potential gains while women are asked how quickly they can get to breakeven. The research is more exhaustive than this summary statement, and it paints a bleak picture for female entrepreneurs in my opinion. It is fascinating how deep our own biases go and how hard it is to break the pattern. Being aware of an inherent bias is the first step to changing behavior.

After I read the study, I wasn't surprised that my board had been using the exact same words recorded in this research. I sent the research study around to the board members. I asked them to read it and reassess how they thought about The RealReal. They did read it, and at least two of them came back to me and said that I was right. The good news is that they were open to looking at their own behavior. We were in this together, and we were all learning as The RealReal was becoming a juggernaut.

What a contrast to The RealReal postpublic board. At year ten, I was thankful that I had the opportunity to work with people who believed in the mission of The RealReal in the beginning and helped make something that started in my kitchen in 2011 amazing. It was ten years of fun, hard work, and amazing people who were on a mission to change the world. Damn, it felt good.

We could only reflect for a moment because we had a lot of work to do to get back in growth mode as the pandemic waned. Starting up again was much harder than shutting down. It felt like our business was trudging through mud. The world felt like that, too.

New York City was a barometer of The RealReal's health, and it was slow to come back. The company's recovery and then subsequent growth were dependent on New York City's recovery. If the city didn't come back, we needed to find other opportunities to grow.

Why was growth necessary? The company's path to profitability depended on it. We had already had one layoff. The next one would be deeper, more painful, and disruptive to the business.

To offset the NYC dependency and because they seemed to be getting to profitability quickly, The RealReal began opening more neighborhood stores. Palo Alto, Austin, Brooklyn, Newport Beach all opened quickly. The larger San Francisco and Chicago stores were still struggling, but so were the shopping areas where they were located. Lines formed outside every store because of the capacity restrictions. I would often stand in a line at a store to understand how everyone was treated. Were they offered coffee or water if it was a store that supplied beverages? Were the security guards inviting and the person in charge of keeping the legal capacity welcoming people when they finally made it to the front of the line? These little things aren't little at all. They help create a better experience for the customer and reinforce the brand. The RealReal wasn't just a luxury resale business; it was luxury resale in an approachable manner.

I made my first trip to the Phoenix operations center in March of 2021. I was greeted in the parking lot by the head of operations security. The 600,000-square-foot facility was still under construction. The front was being built out as offices and training rooms along with a large cafeteria. The balance would house a fine jewelry and watch authentication area eight times bigger than our first warehouse/operations center, and then receiving, authentication, and inventory. Five years before, the emptiness of a facility that size scared me. Now, looking at its vastness, I knew it would fill up quickly. It was only slightly bigger than the facility we had in Perth Amboy, New Jersey, and that one was overflowing with products. Our goal was to open it in September and have the California operations center vacated completely by October. All was on track.

In late April, I was notified that I was chosen to be part of the inaugural list of 50 Women over 50, an initiative started by Mika Brzezinski of *Morning Joe* and *Forbes* magazine to celebrate women over fifty doing amazing things in the world across multiple disciplines. I was totally taken aback by this and honored. It was so secretive that we couldn't even know who the other women were. Then, to my astonishment, *Forbes* put me on the cover in June. I was on one of four covers. The other three were Shonda Rhimes, Kamala Harris, and Cathie Wood.

The magazine was released around the same time my father was in hospice. His mind was clear, but his body was failing. He asked me to bring him a copy of the magazine. I hadn't packed one, but surprisingly I found all four covers at the local Springfield, Illinois, Barnes & Noble. He read it, and tears rolled down his cheek. He told me he was proud of me, and then he said the picture didn't look like me at all. More proof that I photograph beyond recognition, or in this case, might have been photoshopped beyond recognition. When he closed his eyes that night, he never woke up. He was my biggest fan, and once in a while when he was in the mood, he offered me sage advice. He did not like giving his children advice on life as he aged. He liked living, creating, and having fun. He would always tell us we were smart enough to figure things out, and he would add, "I can't live your life or make your choices for you. You have to do what is right for you."

I flew out of Springfield, Illinois, the next morning before he died. When the plane landed in New Jersey, I was informed of my father's passing. I was in my own home, so I opened a bottle of wine, poured a glass, and just sat on my couch looking out the window—the same thing I did when I realized I would no longer be offered a good position in the tech industry. Like then, I didn't cry. I was just numb. Unlike then, I was angry. He had his first heart attack at the age of seventy-two, and instead of treating it as a wake-up call to change his lifestyle, he had gained about eighty pounds over the next ten years. He then had another heart issue, this time heart failure, was revived, and continued his bad habits. He said he was having a "pity party," but he also said he was getting bored with his depression, so he was going to start painting again. He had no interest in talking to a therapist or stopping his nightly cigar smoking. He also developed type 2 diabetes from his weight gain. I was angry at him. He had slowly killed himself. His family and friends had lost a great friend and supporter.

My mother died when I was in my forties. Her life was infinitely sad as a result of her illness. I sobbed when she died. Not because she was gone—she had left us years before because of the impact of the disease on her mind and body. I cried unexpectedly for months because she never had a life.

My father was always there for all of us. He and I had a deep relationship. Even as a kid, I often felt like we were a team. He was my role model for being an entrepreneur. He was my role model for having fun. He was the person I called when something good happened. He was the person I called when I couldn't figure things out. He loved authenticity in people. He loved being an artist. He would often say he beat the odds since it was so hard to make money as an artist. He shunned groupthink and conformity. He was my touchstone for so much goodness, and now he was gone. His humor was with him until the day he passed.

There is a shift that happens when both of your parents are gone. For me it was undefinable at the time, but the feeling that something had shifted was there. I needed to let it exist and take its own shape while I got back to work. I had been at the hospital with my siblings for more than a week. And a board member called repeatedly during that week. He was uneasy about the share price, the management team, the slow growth of the revenue. I was tired. Not a good combination.

I had flown to New York City for a specific reason. I was about to spend some time with an icon. It never occurred to me to reschedule my meeting with Diane von Furstenberg, which was scheduled for the day after my father died. We were filming a video together. This had been planned for months, and I didn't want to reschedule for fear it would never happen. And I didn't want to sit in my anger and sublimated grief.

I met Diane at her office on a Monday in June. I was dressed in a DVF wrap dress purchased on The RealReal and had lots of bangles on my arms. Her handler was thrilled. She said Diane would be happy about my look, too.

The meeting and conversation were a relief and fun and, of course, interesting. She appears fearless. She is also stunning and relaxed.

"You don't look anything like your pictures," she said, kicking off her shoes and relaxing deep in her chair.

"What do you mean?" I fished a bit. "Oh, do I look a lot thinner than I photograph?"

"No, that isn't it." I came close to snorting when I laughed. I mean, could she be more honest? I instantly loved her.

After the interview ended, we ate lunch in her office. She went digging into my past and my family dynamics. Like many families, my family was deeply divided by the Trump presidency, so the stories were rich, somewhat entertaining, and somewhat sad. We ended our brief meeting with her giving me her cell phone number and saying I could call or text her anytime. I have texted her a few times, and she always responds quickly.

I needed to fly back to San Francisco right after our filming. The earnings call was coming up, and I was still rebuilding our staff. We had just hired a recruiting firm for the executives we needed to replace.

Chapter 15

Sometimes They Are Out to Get You

I watched a documentary on Gloria Steinem on a long flight from New York to San Francisco in late July of 2021. As a child, I had three role models: Gloria Steinem, Jane Goodall, and the fictional crime-solving, adventurous young woman Nancy Drew. I had met Jane Goodall at the *Vanity Fair* conference. I fan-girled all over her, she acted bored with me, and then I became embarrassed, took a photo with her, and moved on. It was a disappointing moment, but it didn't dull my image of her. She had probably heard it all before, and I was probably a little boring. Fawning over a famous person can do that.

After watching the documentary on Gloria, I reached out to her people via email, explained Gloria's impact on my life, and asked if we could meet. Within a few days, I had a response. Gloria would love to meet with me. We met for the first time on September 13 at her home and working office on the Upper East Side of New York City. I had just left the grand opening of the Phoenix operations center and was excited to be able to take a moment to meet her.

We spent nearly two hours together talking over a broad range of subjects. A crew was filming every minute. She was so engaging, and her life is so big, it was an honor to spend any time with her. She has a perspective that is sometimes lost. Her knowledge of worldwide cultures and the historical impact of government and religion on women was eye-opening. We would meet again later for a filmed fireside chat at my place in New York City. It was a highlight of my life to meet her. Seeing her on television discussing women's rights when I was young opened my eyes to what was possible. She made sense to me. She represented a type of woman I wanted to become. I wanted to join her in her fights, but I was still in middle school.

I left my meeting with Gloria to fly to Italy for a long-delayed vacation. I wanted to be in great shape mentally and emotionally when I met our new CFO, who was starting in October. I felt like I was getting a good finance partner to drive the company to success.

Our core management team was always in the office, and we had our desks moved so we could communicate easier. I was excited to be coming into the office again. Most employees came back on Wednesdays, but it was hard to get everyone back in the office. The RealReal's corporate offices were open plan, meaning the space had no internal walls. Desks were arranged by functional area. Conference rooms were around the perimeter and there were small two-person meeting rooms for calls or quick one-on-ones. We had taken the sixth and fourth floors on Francisco Street in San Francisco for our corporate office. The sixth floor had an unobstructed view of San Francisco Bay from the Golden Gate Bridge to the Bay Bridge. The south side of the floor faced Coit Tower. The views were breathtaking and always changing with the fog rolling in, the cruise ships docking, the container ships heading toward Oakland, the regattas on Fridays. The view always relaxed me. Just five minutes of taking in the sea air or watching the activity on the bay would allow me to regain perspective.

I really wanted to get people back into the office. The magic that happened through casual and even structured conversations wasn't happening. People were still working hard and solving problems remotely, but the innovative thinking that had driven the company forward by leaps and bounds was nonexistent. The vibe and the work coming out of the teams felt like wash, rinse, repeat. People were tired. The women with children were especially tired. They were still waiting for schools to reopen. Survey after survey of our employee base showed that while people liked the idea of coming back into the office, no one wanted to come back into the office full time. One board member was extremely irritated by this and felt it was due to a lack of leadership—clearly mine. It never mattered that this was a universal problem, nor did it matter that the company had accomplished miracles during the shutdowns.

But over time, many people were choosing to be in the office at least four days a week. The core executive team and I were developing a good working relationship. The new CFO was diving in deeply and remodeling the business. He was also getting to know the members of the board, spending time with the chair of the audit committee and others on the board. Some of the interactions the CFO had with board members were odd enough that he thought something was off. He felt he needed to speak up. Since our desks were next to each other, we would talk regularly, meaning hourly. And, like my relationship with Rati, he was always accessible during nonwork hours to respond to issues that came up. About three months into his job, he started postulating on potential scenarios that could be happening in the background between the board members. He had a feeling that I wasn't in favor with the board and would get fired. Then one of the board members, the one with retail experience, Karen Katz, the former CEO of Neiman Marcus, would step in and run the company. I didn't know the CFO that well, so it was unclear to me if he was astute, paranoid, or both. Turns out he was definitely astute.

I tend to ignore those kinds of projections based on innuendo. It always feels like a conspiracy theory. And it can result in people focusing on the wrong things. The business was demanding. We still were not back to the trends we had seen before COVID. And although we had expanded our store footprint to reenergize growth and increase consignment, the store on Post Street in San Francisco was struggling, as was the one on Michigan Avenue in Chicago. Both had opened at a bad time and had never properly launched. It appeared that both cities were struggling with violence, fentanyl, and homelessness. It felt unsafe to visit either store even during the day. New York City had come back a little faster. It was dirtier than ever, but it felt more resilient and so was our business there. Our consignment levels in Manhattan were climbing and were slightly up when compared to the same period pre-COVID. Not by a lot, but enough to be a positive indicator.

The CFO had hired a new, experienced investor relations professional. They had worked together in his previous position. The RealReal had gone public with an inexperienced public CFO, an inexperienced investor relations person, and an inexperienced public market CEO: me. That never felt like a winning formula. The new CFO brought an enriched skill set to the company and his investor relations person was a good communicator. I felt like I had good partners. The new CFO's theories, specifically those that centered around me being fired, unnerved me, though. His uneasiness had gotten under my skin. To be honest, it reinforced the uneasiness I had been feeling, which had started around the time the CFO joined.

I often took walks with a couple of close friends to talk out issues confidentially. I discussed the board on one of these walks. The board member who had misfired on selling his shares appeared to be working against me in the background. The tone of the board liaison, Rob Krolik, had changed. And Karen Katz, who was a new member of the board and the person the CFO had cited as my heir apparent, was borderline rude to my team and me at board meetings. The other board members seldom talked at the meetings, at least not during the meeting. They always had a meeting after the meeting. That is where decisions seemed to be made. There was something not quite right. I hated the lack of transparency and open communication.

Rob always was a glass-half-empty person and a fan of the exiting CFO, so on a good day, it was hard to know where he was coming from. I did not trust him. I did not trust the motives of the board member who didn't sell his shares, either. As I've mentioned, he most likely had tremendous pressure from his firm to show returns from his prior investment, and if he hadn't sold when the other investors did, he had made a major mistake in my opinion. I say he probably hadn't sold stock because once you are public, there is no transparency around sales and purchases of stock. That is, unless the purchases resulted in a significant ownership position. The RealReal's stock was bouncing all over the place in 2021, as other unprofitable business-to-consumer stocks were doing. The market doesn't like uncertainty, and it felt like uncertain times as we were all figuring out how the economy would perform exiting COVID shutdowns.

We always had a meeting with the finance section of the board and usually a full board meeting prior to an earnings call. We had an earnings call with our investors approximately every three months. I knew something was up with them. To help me sort the board members out,

I had started mapping them to a useful four-quadrant matrix some consultants used when evaluating executives.

I had an opportunity to work with some ex-McKinsey guys who had formed their own company. If you worked with McKinsey, Bain, or any large strategic consultancy in the 1990s and early 2000s, you know they loved a good four-quadrant chart. It is such a flexible device for identifying opportunities, understanding the competition, and explaining complex issues. It was my favorite of their charts, and I still use it when talking to executives.

Again, when you see things that don't make sense in business, you need to follow the money. I've observed that it is always about money or sex or both—but neither would necessarily be transparent to an observer or a business partner.

The consultants had another useful way of looking at people. It reduces people to a four-quadrant chart, which is really reductionist and yet somewhat helpful.

Here is a representation of their four-quadrant people chart:

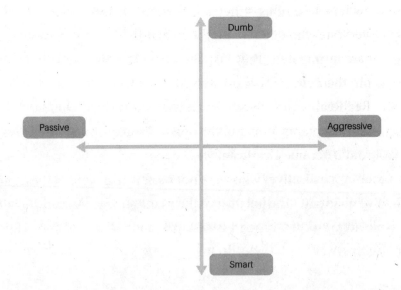

Again, this is a crude generalization, but it mostly works. Who are the most dangerous people you can hire into an organization? Dumb Aggressives—DAs. They tend toward arrogance and never realize their own ignorance. DAs tend to overtake an organization. They are bullies. They dislike transparency in communication. They prefer to give vague answers. They play games. They are value destroyers. They target and try to corral the Smart Passive people, and they are often successful doing so. Smart Passive people don't really want to get involved in company politics. They just want to do their job, and they can be quite introverted. Think of a brilliant engineer who may question things within their area but won't necessarily challenge the leadership. They will eventually quietly quit.

The Smart Aggressives move mountains. They are extremely valuable employees, though may need some leadership training to be less rough around the edges, but these people deliver. They can get taken down by the DAs in the right circumstances, because Smart Aggressives are more prone to getting the right stuff done quickly. They aren't always politically savvy. They are by nature value creators. The DAs don't know how to do that—they are power seekers and tend to work against everyone who doesn't join their alliance. Dumb passives either resign or are terminated. They just don't have the drive or curiosity to exist within their current organization.

The RealReal was a diverse organization. We had some of each type across the organization and the board. I reacquainted myself with the tool, and it became clear what was happening. The board members and a couple of executives who were not performing were in the dumb aggressive quadrant. The balance of the management team, especially me, were acting as smart aggressives and ignoring the politics of the dumb aggressives.

You may want to use this tool to help you understand people. I learned about it early on in my career. I started at Software Publishing Corporation in the early 1980s. It was a vibrant, exciting time as personal computers and software, for these machines were an explosive new business. And I was a vibrant employee in my early twenties who wanted to learn as much as possible. The personal computer software industry was nascent, and the development platforms had not stabilized. A company like Software Publishing had to develop across many versions of DOS, the operating system at the time. This splintered resources and complicated development priorities. Choosing the wrong platform or missing a key version of the operating system could result in the competition taking over.

Software Publishing had made a bet that personal computer software needed to be easy and not feature rich. That turned out to be mostly wrong because the initial business was in corporations. But the company was doing fine. Then an engineer presented a concept of presentation graphics to the management team, the precursor to PowerPoint. Named Harvard Graphics, it was a revolutionary, category-creating breakthrough. This replaced the old slide carousel. The business was on fire, and the trajectory looked compelling. The company needed to develop a professional sales force and hired a key executive from IBM to run it. He was the ultimate in dumb aggressiveness. He knew his field well, but his aspirations were greater than running sales. Prior to his joining, the company resembled a meritocracy and was highly collaborative. The new sales leader managed by exclusion, meaning people became dead to him if they challenged him or his point of view on the company. His star kept rising, and talent kept leaving. The CEO thought this new leader was the answer to becoming a major software player, not just a presentation graphics company. People were afraid to speak against this leader. The result? Most of the talent left, the CEO/

founder resigned, and that was the beginning of the end. One person can make a difference.

As 2021 drew to a close, it was clear I would be battling dumb aggressives in my own company. Unfortunately, I was exhausted, completely bone tired. Still, I loved what I did and was incredibly hopeful about the business. Still, I was so uneasy about the board and the dynamics there, I was getting paranoid. The death of my father also haunted me. I was still angry that my dad, my friend, had chosen not to take care of himself and had died because of that. My feisty dog, Betty, had also died in August. She was nearly seventeen, blind and going deaf, but damn I loved that dog. And I missed her. It was a year of loss with some bright spots. Next year had to be better.

Chapter 16

It's O-V-E-R

I am one of those people who likes to reassess the past year before moving into the next. Nothing formal, nothing dramatic, just some downtime to reflect. It was clear to me that I needed to make some changes in the organization. It was time to promote Rati to president and have her manage the entire operation of the business. She excelled at process and day-to-day management, hired well, understood the key levers of the business, and deserved the promotion.

On the business side, I needed to focus on investors and the board and work on a longer-term financial plan while ensuring we hit our quarterly numbers. The new CFO and I were working well together. His model for the business made sense to me and all executives in the company. He was still learning the nuances of the business, but he was coming up to speed quickly. We had a lot of work to do to get the business on better financial footing. Prior to COVID, the business had been extremely predictable. It was on firm footing and a solid path toward profitability. COVID had altered that path substantially. And we had opened more stores than we had previously planned to, some-what as a reaction to COVID's limits on our ability to generate supply. We needed to assess the store expansion.

Now consumer buying patterns, inflation, fear of a recession, cities flailing, the quiet quitting, and even the threat and reality of the Ukraine war were all affecting businesses. The RealReal was no different.

The board approved Rati's promotion, and the change was made in January. Our fiscal year 2022 budget approval meeting was set for mid-February. This was common practice for us, as it allowed us to close the books from the previous year, finalize a solid plan for the current year based on those results, and then have enough time to prepare for the next earnings call.

During this process, some odd, but perhaps predictable, events started happening. The board member who I suspected did not sell his shares started cutting me out of conversations he was having with the CFO. This made the CFO uneasy, and it was against the bylaws adopted by the board. When I found out, I placed a call to this person. He made himself generally unavailable to me. Two nights before the board meeting, he left a message and said he could meet me late in the evening before the board meeting the next day. I did not get that message in time to respond because of my travel schedule. Somehow, I think he knew it would work out that way.

The February board of directors meeting was held at the Phoenix operations center. It would be the first time any board member had stepped foot in any of our operations centers. The agenda was a tour and then the meeting. Our CFO had been having meetings with as many board members as possible prior to the meeting to walk them through our proposed plan.

The Phoenix operations center is stunning. The marketing and merchandising teams had put branding on the walls to represent The

RealReal's core values. There was a wall-to-wall fashion mural in the cafeteria painted by a local artist. It was the crown jewel in the operations centers for the company. The training was going well with the new hires, so consequently the center was operating at a level ahead of plan. The fine jewelry and watch area was almost as big as our entire Oakdale warehouse all of those years ago. The inbound and outbound operations teams were in place and doing well. The facility sparkled. I was and am a stickler for clean operations centers and employee bathrooms. It was not unusual for me to pick up debris on the floor when I was in our operations center and then let the section manager know they needed to pay attention to cleanliness. I was excited to show the board the work the team had done.

Here is where it all becomes a bit tricky regarding what I can write about legally. Yes, under duress, I signed a nondisclosure agreement with The RealReal. I can tell you that I was ambushed and felt betrayed. Then I lost my temper during the board meeting. Men and older women tend to hate when women lose their temper, even though I know I was cogent in my anger. Still, I gave away my power at that moment. A member of my team said that if a man had done what I did, there would have been no consequences. I kind of think the noose was hung and then I placed my neck in it.

Looking back, the board had probably already reached a conclusion that I had to be removed. And although I have no real information about who was working against me, I clearly have a strong idea. As I have noted before, it most likely was about money. If you follow the money, there is one person who most likely set the wheels in motion. I believe the remaining private equity board member had sown his poisoned seeds. I had inadvertently fed into his story when I lost my temper. If I had to do it all over again, I would have remained detached from the plan that was hatched to oust me and found a way to turn it to my advantage. But I did not react that way. I effing lost it. I had never experienced the type of antics that went on during that board meeting, nor had my integrity been called into question before. The company had just come through an incredibly hard time, and we had risen to the challenge. Instead of recognizing this and giving guidance on the fiscal year 2022 plan, I believe that one person used this time to make a move against me as the leader. I have heard this type of thing many times from others, and it seems incredible, but it is true. It only takes one person working against the CEO to unseat them. But, they did not fire me then. That came later. Here is how it went down.

In that pivotal board meeting, I might or might not have said to the PE guy, "Fuck you, you aren't going to ruin my company." It is possible that Karen Katz said to me that I was not a good leader. It all felt foggy when I left the board meeting. I knew it was bad then, but I did not know how bad it would get.

Fast forward to the first week of June and I am still the CEO trying to make great things happen. A board member, Rob Krolik, reached out and said he was going to stop by for a business update on a Thursday afternoon. When he showed up, he had Caretha Coleman, another board member, with him. Rati, general counsel Todd Suko, the new CFO, and I were in the office. The two board members took a seat in the large glass conference room. Before I joined them, I told Rati and the CFO that this wasn't good. I had always said that everyone reported to someone, and the board had the right to fire the CEO.

Caretha said something like "It is time for you to go." My Apple Watch sent out a loud alert. I had exceeded my maximum heart rate. I dismissed the message.

"Why?" I asked.

"You did not hit your numbers during COVID," Rob replied.

I yelled, *Are you fucking kidding me?* At least I said that in my head. Then they handed me a press release stating that our CFO would be made CEO immediately, along with some documents to sign.

"I need to get a lawyer."

"I don't want to ruin your weekend or anything, but we need this wrapped up quickly," Rob said.

I remember looking at him incredulously and thinking something was clearly wrong with this guy. "Ruin my weekend? You are trying to ruin my life."

Then Rob and Caretha emphasized that I could not tell anyone, including my direct reports, because they did not know. Again, I was incredulous. I pointed out that we were sitting in a glass conference room, and during the course of our conversation, each one of them had walked past the conference room and looked into it to see my facial expression, which was not a happy one.

"I am telling the executives. There is no way I am going out there and lying to them," I said.

"Well, you have to tell us after you tell them."

"Fine, I'll tell them within minutes after you leave."

They left. I told my team. The CFO was shocked because no one asked him if he wanted to be the interim CEO. He did not. Todd was shocked because he was the general counsel of a public company and did not know what was happening. Rati was demoralized because she read the press release. I was crying. So were others.

My bet was that one of the board members wanted to call the shots and thought our CFO was his guy to work through. However, that was not exactly how it played out. The CFO and general counsel requested a board call the following Friday morning. Their goal was to have Rati be co-CEO. The CFO knew he needed an expert operator to run the company. Rati was already doing it as president. Also, he had his paranoia hat on, I am sure. He had told me he never trusted the board members. Turns out, he was right to feel that way. The board, under duress, gave Rati the co-CEO title. A board member required that the co-CEO's meet with him weekly. This board member had some things he wanted them to implement.

And after the announcement that I was stepping down and leaving was made, I had only a couple of work requirements within the company before the year 2022 ended. I was in deep pain the entire time, but I needed to say yes to anything requested of me. The most fun thing I did was attend the event for the top salespeople, called the Elite Club. Every year, the event is held at a world-class hotel. The top salespeople can enjoy prepaid spa sessions, and activities like ziplining, yoga, and hiking in the morning. There are talks during the day and amazing food at night. Before I was fired, this was one of my favorite events of the year. This year was more than a little different. It was stressful and extremely sad. I had to be less than honest with the team there and yet supportive and encouraging—all the while knowing that it was going to be a rocky, uncertain time. It made me sick to my stomach to act like all was fine. I ended up changing the subject about my impending departure every time the subject was raised.

As the end of December 2022 neared, I was staying at my place in New York City. A stone had fallen out from a ring I had purchased at The RealReal, and I had reached out to the head of the fine jewelry and watch department to see how it could be repaired. I had been instructed to drop it off at The RealReal Madison Avenue store with specific instructions on who it needed to be sent to at the operations center.

I brought it to the store, and no one on the first floor recognized me. I asked to speak to the store manager and explained my situation. I did not mention that I was the founder or the former CEO and technically was still an employee. The store manager had no idea who I was. Even when I gave her my email address to verify that I had made the purchase of the ring, it didn't register with her. When she said what she was going to do with the ring, I corrected her and said that she needed to send it to this specific person at this specific location. I then gave her the phone number and email address of the person she needed to speak with to correct my issue. After about thirty minutes, the ordeal was over, and I left the store.

Clearly, my time at The RealReal was fleeting. I was no longer on the website, and the history had been erased. Just like that, I was nothing. What did I do after I vomited around the corner? I called Rati and asked her to get me back on the website and gave her the name of the store manager who clearly would have done the wrong thing for any customer. The website information was later restored, but at that moment, the nausea and the pain were too great.

About two months later, after the new CEO was announced, I received a call from another CEO in the fashion industry.

"I just saw the announcement. The Board of Directors hired a tire sales guy."

"He was unemployed at the time."

"So, an unemployed guy who used to sell tires for a living."

"And has never been a CEO."

"How are you doing?"

"Better, love you," I said, laughing. "Thanks."

And that is exactly who the board hired. The new hire had worked with a board member before at another company. They had left the company as it slipped into bankruptcy. That company was now in a turnaround mode and it had filed for Chapter 11 bankruptcy. Then he had gone on to work for a tire company for a bit. When The

RealReal board of directors interviewed him for the position, he was unemployed.

It is an interesting emotional, physical, and mental challenge when something you love and have created is taken away from you. Especially for me, because it was the first thing I thought of when I woke up and the last thing I thought about when I went to bed for more than eleven years.

I knew I could not have regular contact with the employees, especially the management team. For my own mental health, I limited any future conversations with the executives, especially Rati. She and I had talked all the time every day. I missed her and the business immensely, but I knew it would mentally damage me to keep myself attached. I did kind of love it when the CFO would call and give me his point of view, though, especially when the new CEO joined. Let's just say they did not get along. The CFO left in late 2023. It was a mutual decision.

I also exercised more than normal. That was my stress relief. And for a month or so, I cried every day when I worked out. Then my mood shifted as I worked out, and I enjoyed envisioning the board members having something terrible happening to them and their careers. Some days when I was working out, I envisioned the board members spontaneously combusting. This always made me laugh, because when I was a kid, the grocery store magazine racks near the checkout always reported a story of someone who had spontaneously combusted. I still remember one spontaneous combustion photo that showed two charred ankles with no body above them. The feet were still there, and they had on socks and shoes that oddly were not charred. I thought about them like this for a few weeks. Then my mood shifted again to thinking about my future and not really caring what happened to the board members, just hoping that Rati stayed on at The RealReal so it would have great stewardship.

I planned my move to Los Angeles and started working on a concept for my next adventure, which I had explored during COVID.

I also analyzed what I did incorrectly because, clearly, I contributed to my own demise. Here are my conclusions: I did not recommend board members that matched the values of The RealReal. Further, only one of them had any understanding of the dynamics of a high-growth, category-busting company. These people had never created a business or worked in an entrepreneurial company, let alone one that was based on technology. And I was so busy running the company that I didn't spend enough time with the new board members to bring them up to speed and help them understand the company. Ultimately, I did not respect them, and that showed. Also, I should have been conscious of competing motives at the board level. I'm not sure I could have maneuvered around those well, however. When a board member wants the CEO out and that board member can persuade others, the CEO is doomed.

I attended two more meetings with board members present after *the* board meeting at the operations center. One with the entire management team, including some of the younger directors in the company. That was a virtual meeting, and a few of the board comments made during the meeting were demoralizing to some of the executives. I gave the board the feedback that those comments should have been said to me after the meeting, not during the meeting when young directors were present. They did not appreciate my commenting on their behavior. I really believed and had evidence by then that they were hierarchical in their thinking and above feedback. So, I clearly had a death wish. Or on some level, I already knew it was over.

Also, one could argue that it was time for me to go. I know I would have positively engaged in the succession discussion that was scheduled to happen in August. Succession planning was required by our charter and is normal for a public company. This planning had a sub-committee that would do the work and report back to the board. The succession committee's responsibility was primarily to ensure a smooth transition when any key executives left. That meeting never happened. And my recommendations would have been ignored anyway because the discussions that were happening behind closed doors were clearly not supportive of me and my point of view.

Life is so short and experiences like The RealReal so rare and wonderful. Ultimately, I had to take joy in what had happened in my life and find ways to move on to something else. I've never lived in the past, and for a few months I was fighting like hell not to get sucked into that way of thinking. We are all in control of our own thoughts. I had to fight mine to keep in the positive direction while also honoring the grief I felt.

Before I started The RealReal, I often spoke at events about Pets.com and the lessons I learned after that failure. Once after my talk, for which I received a standing ovation, the host came up to the microphone to sum up my presentation. "We have just heard from someone who, like Icarus, flew too close to the sun, and look what happened to her." I wondered if she was channeling Dana Carvey's Church Lady, but no, she was serious.

The Icarus story is one of hubris and complacency. Icarus was not an entrepreneur. This is an entrepreneur's story. However, like Icarus, I have had prolonged moments of hubris—especially if hubris is defined as excessive self-confidence. What entrepreneur hasn't? And, in many cases, that self-confidence was replaced by doubt and then self-confidence would bounce back again because doubt doesn't get you anywhere. But I have never suffered from complacency.

I would rather reach high and fail then never strive to be the best I could be. Francis Ford Coppola has a good saying to keep in mind: "I think it's better to be overly ambitious and fail than to be under ambitious and succeed in a mundane way."

Then this happened, which made me very happy: John Kroyl was fired as CEO of The RealReal in October 2024. His tenure was less than two years. Rati Sahi Levesque was promoted to CEO. The announcement was made on October 28, 2024.

Chapter 17

New Beginnings

During COVID, I became extremely interested in nutrition and how our genes impact how nutrients are absorbed. I was sure that there was a connection between one's genes and illness that could be prevented by changing our diet. Reading published articles reinforced that we can all alter how our genes present, meaning you can alter your health by good and bad habits. Simply said, your genetic tendencies can be altered by lifestyle choices—some refer to this as turning on genes due to lifestyle choices. Then there is the oft-used phrase "your genes are not your destiny"—a phrase backed by science. And, since we are all different, I was interested in understanding what I personally needed to eat to optimize my health.

I contacted a medical doctor I had known for years who had decided years ago to focus her practice on preventative care, specifically nutrition. She had me take three tests. First, I took a nutrition genetic test that specifically looked at how my genes absorb nutrients. Then I took an epigenetic test that measured how my cells were aging.

Last, I took a biometric test to understand my vitamin D and omega-3 levels. Once the doctor received my results, she consulted with other genetic experts and cross-referenced various research studies and gave me a consultation that was illuminating. Specifically, my body does not absorb omega-3s well at all. This somewhat explained why I had a bad reaction to eating fatty fish, like salmon. The biomarker test also revealed that I had low omega-3s in my blood. Because omega-3s are very important for heart health and brain health, I started supplementation to offset my issue. There were other findings, too, that could be corrected through diet.

The process the doctor went through to validate my genetic information, which furthered her deep understanding of the nutrients I was missing to make a recommendation just for me, felt like it could be put into an algorithm and commercialized.

I kept discussing this idea with her during COVID. I also started trying other nutrition solutions that were on the market, many of which had some of the components of testing that I had done with this doctor. In fact, it got a little strange at one point because I kept showing up at the Quest Diagnostics near my home in Marin County to have my blood drawn. It was one of those scenarios where the receptionist clearly appeared a little suspicious when she would welcome me back every ten days. This was also the time of mandated mask wearing. At some point, the phlebologist asked me if I was well, as she had taken my blood over three times in four weeks for various services. I also heard a lot about the emotional and physical adjustments she was making after weight-loss surgery.

So as all of the craziness was going on at The RealReal, I was getting interested in starting a new company. I was also getting tired of living in the Bay Area. I no longer wanted to live with cold summers and in the center of the tech universe. I wanted to move somewhere sunnier in California. I had spent a great deal of time in Los Angeles over the past ten years because of its importance to The RealReal and felt comfortable with it. I kind of liked it and thought I'd like living there for a while.

The stage was being set for my next chapter. I was excited about the thought of starting another company and had a deep passion for what was shaping up to be Ahara. Having said that, I never wanted to totally leave The RealReal. And I never would have done so on my own.

But I did have to leave The RealReal, and that gave me time to continue to explore personalized and precision nutrition. About three months after my The RealReal exit, I had a few meetings with Dana Settle of Greycroft about this concept. Greycroft became the first investor in Ahara, and we launched the product into beta in the fall of 2023 with the doctor as the cofounder.

A new journey began.

Chapter 18

Ahara in the Wild

A hara received over \$10 million in funding between 2022 and 2023. The next step was hiring the team to execute the vision. That team consisted of a chief data scientist, a sports nutrition expert, a head of product management, a head of product development, a head of marketing, and a chief medical officer with a strong social following. It took more than one year from the original funding date to bring the product to market. Ahara launched in August 2023 in beta.

The product is designed with a scientifically valid algorithm to diagnose deficiencies in a person's key nutrients after the person takes a health survey. Those nutrient deficiencies are directly linked to key symptoms. Then an individual is given a list of optimal foods they should eat to offset their nutrient deficiencies and personalized recipes. Further, supplements are recommended when food alone will not meet the person's nutrients needs. For example, vitamin D, a nutrient many people are low in, cannot be found in food. Therefore, supplementation is often necessary. The product also has a testing level for more precise nutritional guidance. It tests how you absorb nutrients, your internal rate of aging, and your omega-3 and vitamin D levels.

The product gained some traction in its first few weeks but not enough. We then began experimenting with different pricing schemes. Small upgrades were added to the product, and we began deeper user testing. The user testing we conducted showed a few key trends. TikTok and Instagram influencers give nutritional guidance that is sometimes not exactly good science or, worse yet, just bad science. It has had a significant influence on people's general perception of how to eat for their health. Breaking these various preconceptions is very hard, if not impossible. That perception is taken to the extreme by biohackers who want to live forever or at least a very long time. These people use their bodies as a testing device and try injectable growth hormones, injectable peptides, different compounded supplements, odd exercise devices, brain stimulators, and so on. And they have big followings. They think of themselves as being on the forefront of science. Maybe they are, but they may also be on the forefront of bad health.

It became clear by the end of 2023 that we had to focus on selling into the corporate market as a benefit to employees and that we had to decrease our burn rate, or our expenses per month. The doctor left the company, and the data scientist and the product manager, along with another employee, were put on part time for three months.

Ahara was approved by Anthem as a benefit for their members. Some key insurance agencies told us that they were struggling with how to approve the prescription of the weight loss drugs. They wanted Ahara to focus on nutritional consulting for weight loss patients prior to putting them on the weight loss drugs. We launched a weight loss vertical that addresses this concern by offering nutritional consulting before, during, and after a person uses a weight loss drug. We are also collaborating with a medical doctor group to offer the compounded versions of the weight loss drugs to our base.

In closing, here is one of my favorite quotes—but modified a bit.

It is not the critic who counts; not the man who points out how the strong [woman] stumbles, or where the doer of deeds could have done them better. The credit belongs to the [woman] who is actually in the arena, whose face is marred by dust and sweat and blood; who strives valiantly; who errs, who comes up short again and again, because there is no effort without error and shortcoming; but who does actually strive to do the deeds; who knows great enthusiasms, the great devotions; who spends [herself]in a worthy cause;.who at the best knows in the end the triumph of high achievement, and who at the worst, if [she] fails, at least [she] fails while daring greatly, so that [her] place shall never be with those cold and timid souls who neither know victory nor defeat.

—Theodore Roosevelt
(gender modification by Julie Wainwright)

Acknowledgments

This book would not have happened if Kathy Schneider, my literary agent, would not have worked hard to make it happen. She was on my team and each rejection (yes, we had a few) she met with optimism that the book would land with the right publisher. Her guidance helped me immensely. She also encouraged me to write my own story after some failed attempts with ghostwriters. My lawyer, Kim Schelfler, was also extremely resourceful and made a big difference.

Then there is the BenBella team and their interesting, progressive business model for authors—their approach just makes sense. Thankfully, they introduced me to Camille Cline, my book editor, who made the book even better. Victoria Carmody got it over the finish line, and Glenn Yeffeth believed in the book from the beginning.

In life, I have to acknowledge my great friends and family (in no particular order): Kenny, Cheryl, Shannon, Kathryn (may you rest in peace), Julie times two, Ann, Nancy, Amy, Magdalena, Fred, Judy, Tom, Sonja, Carol, Dana, Lorrie, Marilyn, Jimbo, and Janer. You all are so different and so wonderful. Thank you.

Lastly, at The RealReal, thank you to all of the people I worked with day in and day out. We were on a magnificent, mission-driven journey together, and it was an honor to work with you. Well, not all of you—some of you were very bad actors. Still, even you, the bad actors, are teachers, so I am thankful for that.

And I will close with an even bigger thanks to the early investors, Maha, Dana, Mathias, Keval, Cynthia, and Mike. Thank you for helping build an amazing brand that changed the fashion industry, helped people understand the positive climate impact of recirculating goods, and forever changed the way people shop.

Appendix

An Entrepreneur's Checklist,
for the Crazy Greats Who Do It

The odds of being a successful entrepreneur are really low. If you google the odds, you will see that 90 percent of start-ups fail. Now, if you are starting a technology business and you are a woman, your likelihood of getting financed from a venture capitalist is very low. The number when I started writing this book was just under 3 percent. Now, it is just under 2 percent. Women venture capitalists now make up 11 percent of all venture capitalists, but according to the *Harvard Business Review* research published on June 17, 2017, women bring the same bias to the investing table that men do. If you are a person of color, your chance of getting funding is less than 1 percent. Admittedly, these numbers are all grim and off-putting.

But so what? If you have a great idea, in an area people care about, and you execute it better than anyone, then you need to try to do your business. Maybe you will fail. And you might think that everyone is judging you for failing. Let's say many are doing that, but my bet is the people judging you have never taken a risk in their life. And, anyway, they are not living your life. You are.

Here are some considerations for your concept:

- Are you creating a new concept or entering an existing market?
- Do you have trusted friends you can call on? You might have noticed that without my friends, I never could have made The RealReal a success.
- What is your unique selling proposition, and does it matter to your target audience?
- Can you test your idea or concept with minimal cash?
- Have you done profit and loss projections for your business? What is the capital required?
- Do you have access to capital if you need it? How long can you live without a salary?
- Is this the right time in your life to set a business as your top priority? Do you need a steady job? Do you have other demands that will take away from your ability to get a new venture off the ground?
- Do you understand technology and how to apply it to your business (because every business is a technology business now)? If you do not, consider hiring a technology person who can also set up your data tables for daily relevant information early in the formation of your company.
- Can you build a good team? Are you clear on your values as an employer and what values you want in your employees? As you can see from my experience at The RealReal, people make all the difference and alignment of values is critical.

- Can you make decisions with limited data points? Can you be decisive? Even bad decisions are better than no decisions at all.
- Are you comfortable analyzing data? It is important that you understand the implications behind the trends so you can iterate quickly if you need to do so.
- Do you need a cofounder? What skill sets should a cofounder bring to the business?
- Are you passionate about what you will be working on? Passion will carry you when the emotional and physical fatigue sets in.
- How's your mental health? Start-ups take a toll on your psyche. There are lots of ups and downs. You will hear more noes than yeses. It will be demoralizing.
- How's your physical health? You will need a lot of energy.
- Do you know how to ask people for help and network when needed?
- You must know when to hold them and when to fold them. What I mean by that is how will you know that your business is successful? What data points will you put in place to know this? What if it is not successful—how will you know?
- What is the environmental impact of your business? How will you positively contribute to the planet? I have seen so many fashion start-ups for clothing, jewelry, or makeup that have a significantly negative impact on the planet. The planet does not need more throwaway stuff or excess packaging. You can design a business that is a positive contributor to the environment. Please do so.
- Do you want to build a local business or a national business? In any case, knowing your local community leaders is

important, even if they are inept. Better to know who you are
dealing with, and most people in service to the community
want to help new businesses. Also consider working with your
local community leaders for job fairs and community events.
Participating and leading in the community online or locally
are important as you grow.

- Do you have a good sense of humor? You will need it, and
  it makes any start-up a lot more fun. It doesn't hurt in life,
  either.

About the Author

Julie Wainwright is the CEO and cofounder of Ahara, a personalized nutrition company that launched in late 2023, and one of the most successful business leaders in the world. An entrepreneur and e-commerce pioneer, she has been at the helm of leading tech and consumer companies for more than twenty years and is one of only twenty-three women to found and lead a company through an IPO.

In 2011, she founded the billion-dollar company The RealReal, forever changing the way people buy and sell high-end luxury. Wainwright raised sizable venture capital funding and took the company public in 2019. Prior to The RealReal, she was CEO of Reel.com and Pets.com. She is the recipient of numerous awards including *Entrepreneur*'s 50 Most Daring Entrepreneurs, *Inc.*'s Female Founders 100 List, *Fast Company*'s Most Creative People in Business, and *Vanity Fair*'s New Establishment List, and was selected for the inaugural *Forbes* 50 Over 50 List (2021), and made the cover of *Forbes* in June 2021. She has also been featured in the *New York Times*, *Women's Wear Daily*, *Vogue Business*, the *Wall Street Journal*, and *Smart Company* and on *CNBC*, *Fox Business*, *Fox News Radio*, and podcasts including *Bloomberg*'s Studio. Wainwright is a frequent speaker at business events such as the

Forbes Women's Summit, *Vanity Fair*'s New Establishment Summit, the *New York Times* Luxury Summit, and many more.

She is an advisor and supporter of nonprofits focused on sustainability, women, children, and the arts, including Cora, a San Mateo California agency for those affected by intimate partner abuse, MOCA where she sits on the Board of Directors, various animal shelters and pet foster organizations, and Purdue's Mitchell E. Daniels Jr. School of Business. She has established scholarships at Purdue for women in business and at Parsons School of Design for students studying sustainable fashion. She is a board member of Inspirato. Wainwright is a graduate of Purdue University. She lives in Los Angeles and New York.